A. J. Cook

LIVES of the LEFT is a new series of original biographies of leading figures in the European and North American socialist and labour movements. Short, lively and accessible, they will be welcomed by students of history and politics and by anyone interested in the development of the Left.

general editor   David Howell

published: *J. Ramsay MacDonald* Austen Morgan
James Maxton William Knox
Karl Kautsky Dick Geary
'Big Bill' Haywood Melvyn Dubofsky
A. J. Cook Paul Davies
R. H. Tawney Anthony Wright

forthcoming, to include: *Aneurin Bevan* Dai Smith
Thomas Johnston Graham Walker
Eugene Debs Gail Malmgreen
Ernest Bevin Peter Weiler

A. J. Cook

Paul Davies

Manchester University Press

Published by Manchester University Press, Oxford Road,
Manchester, M13 9PL, UK

British Library cataloguing in publication data
Davies, Paul, *1951-*
    A. J. Cook. — (Lives of the left).
    1. Cook, A. J. 2. Miners' Federation of Great Britain—Biography
    3. Trade-unions—Great Britain—officials and employees—Biography
    I. Title   II. Series
    331.88'092'4   HD6665.C5/

ISBN 0 7190 2160 X *hardback*
ISBN 0 7190 2161 8 *paperback*

Set in Perpetua
by Koinonia Ltd, Manchester

Printed in Great Britain
by Robert Hartnoll (1985) Ltd, Bodmin, Cornwall

Contents

1 From the Mendips to the Rhondda

Selina Brock was a remarkable woman. When twelve years old she lost a leg in an accident, but this did not prevent her becoming an apprentice dressmaker and, by her late teens, a self-employed dressmaker with her own cottage. At the age of nineteen she married a thirty-year-old soldier by the name of Tom Cook. In November 1883 the Cooks were in Wookey, a small village approximately three miles west of Wells, at the southern extreme of the Mendip Hills, in the heart of the glorious Somerset countryside. On 22 November Selina Cook gave birth to the first of her ten children. The birth was registered in Wells on New Year's Day 1884, and the child was named Arthur James. It was into this overwhelmingly agricultural environment that one of the most fascinating figures in British labour history was born.

The early years of Arthur Cook's life may have owed their geographical location to the varying deployment of his father's regiment, but Selina Cook was the real formative influence on her son. A deeply religious woman, Selina led her family out of the Church of England and into Baptist nonconformity; furthermore she was involved in the nascent Salvation Army. Such convictions were passed on to all her children, and were likely to instil in Arthur Cook a sensitivity towards injustice and a desire for social reform and improvement. The roots of his later socialism were grounded in the humanitarianism to which he was exposed as a child. Although eventually he rejected the chapel, he remained a Christian all his life.

Following Tom Cook's retirement from the army, the family settled in the idyllic village of Cheddar. The Cooks bought a house in Silver Street and established a small market gardening business. At the back of the house a large double gate led up into the Mendips. Arthur attended the Cheddar National School and did well. But his life was not the paradise it might appear. His relationship with his father, never good, worsened as more children arrived. By 1896, when Arthur was twelve, the strain was bad enough to prompt Selina Cook to ask a local dairy farmer and a fellow Baptist by the name of Caleb Durbin to take Arthur on as a labourer. Durbin agreed, and Cook moved the short distance to his farm, sleeping there in order to rise early to milk cows.

Arthur Cook testified later to the influence Caleb Durbin had on his development, observing that 'the farmer for whom I went to work was my real schoolmaster'.[1] Durbin possessed a large library; he started Arthur's reading with Smiles's *Self Help* and followed with Shakespeare, Ruskin, Cobden and Bright. Cook described Durbin as 'a radical – almost the only radical in a village of Tories', but *religion* rather than politics dominated Arthur Cook's teens, and it was his rapid advancement within the Baptist movement that provided the first clue that Cook was no ordinary farm labourer. Prompted, no doubt, by Selina Cook and Caleb Durbin, Arthur became a boy preacher of local notoriety, touring the chapels delivering his own sermons to Sunday Schools and adult congregations. It seems evident that Cook, like many other trade union leaders, gained his first experience as an orator in the chapel pulpit.

When Arthur Cook was seventeen he was offered a place at a Baptist college to train for the ministry. According to Cook's sister Louise, this would have pleased their mother, but Cook had already decided to leave Somerset and travel to South Wales to work in the coal mines. The reason for Cook's decision seems to have been overwhelmingly pecuniary. In 1926 he recollected that Durbin could not afford to pay good wages, and that in any case farm work 'did not attract me'. Cook also recalled that his father had been ill for some time and 'my mother was carrying the burden of a large family'. Cook was set to join a mass migration from the agricultural fringes of south-western England into the booming South Wales coalfield. From Somerset alone in the 1890s an average of a thousand boys a year were sucked into Glamorgan by the attraction of pit work and higher earnings. With £5 saved up and his box full of sermons, Arthur Cook left with some friends for the Rhondda valleys. The year was 1901 and he was seventeen years old; Arthur Cook was to spend the next twenty years of his working life underground.

It would be difficult to exaggerate the contrast between Wookey or Cheddar and Arthur Cook's new world in Porth. Situated at the conjunction of the two Rhondda valleys, Porth in many ways exemplified the metamorphosis of the Rhondda. By 1901 Porth had changed rapidly from a village into a dynamic coal-town of some 20,000 people. The pace of growth was such that Porth exhibited all the problems common to frontier towns: a survey of the local press of the 1900s reveals that Porth was dogged by housing shortages, inadequate street-lighting, deficient sanitation and a lack of recreational facilities.

The forty years prior to the Great War witnessed a spectacular rush for Rhondda coal. By the turn of the century the expansion of the industry was reaching its climax. The valleys had been transformed from pasture to the most intensely mined area in Britain. Contemporary photographs indicate how this sudden explosion produced a uniquely cramped environment with the collieries, roads, rivers and railway lines threaded along the valley floors, forcing the housing onto the hillsides in terraced ribbons. As industry expanded, the communities which accompanied each colliery fused to form *the* Rhondda, two bands of habitation and hardware stretching from Blaenrhondda at the head of the Rhondda Fawr and from Maerdy at the top of the Rhondda Fach to their merger at Porth. If we are to empathise with A. J. Cook, and if we are to understand his development as a leader of men, we must remember that he was a product of this unique environment. The Rhondda of the 1900s was a crowded, noisy, fast-moving place; as Dai Smith has eloquently put it, 'the Society had the stumbling vitality of a blind man on a spree'.[2]

When Arthur Cook arrived in Porth he found work quickly at the Trefor Colliery in Trehafod. He was also fortunate enough to find lodgings with a fellow miner and Baptist. The Trefor pit was a steam colliery sunk in the early 1880s by William Thomas Lewis (later Lord Merthyr), and Cook's arrival in Porth coincided with the amalgamation of four local collieries under Lewis's ownership, forming the nucleus of one of the largest mining enterprises in Great Britain, the Lewis-Merthyr Collieries Company Limited. In the boom conditions of the time Arthur Cook, like many new recruits to the industry, was immediately put to work underground as labourer and apprentice collier. He came face to face at once with the harsh realities of life underground. On his first day at the coal-face (an alarming experience in its own right) a man working an adjacent stall was killed by a fall of stone, and Cook helped to carry the man's body to the surface and home to his wife and children. Not surprisingly, the incident left a deep impression on the seventeen-year-old Cook. He had learnt that there was blood on the coal.

Despite the horrors of this baptism Cook made good progress at his work. He graduated quickly from labourer to haulier, and then went on to become a collier with a stall of his own. He worked hard and earned enough to send money home to his mother and save some besides. This achievement was made easier by Cook's teetotalism, while no doubt he was given greater resolve by his plans to marry Annie Edwards, the daughter of his landlord.

By 1906, when he married Annie, Cook had saved £100 with which to furnish the small house they rented from the Lewis–Merthyr company.

Outside working hours Cook's life continued to be dominated by religion. He attended the Baptist chapel in Porth, preached and became a Sunday School teacher and a deacon. Some of his most vivid recollections of this period concerned the remarkable Welsh religious revival of 1904-5. Starting inauspiciously in the village of Loughor near Llanelli in south-west Glamorgan, under the leadership of Evan Roberts, the revival swept across industrial South Wales, reaching Porth in November 1904. Its impact, though brief, was dramatic. Prayer meetings were held underground in the pits, while at the end of their shift many miners ignored the temptations of food and rest and headed for the nearest chapel. And Arthur Cook, aged twenty-one, was himself caught up in the fervour: 'To me, an ardent young preacher, the Revival, whilst it lasted, was all I thought worth living for; it filled my thoughts and kept me tense and absorbed.'

When Cook began work at the Trefor colliery he joined the South Wales Miners Federation (SWMF) which had been founded in 1898. For nearly five years, however, such was his commitment to Baptism, he remained unaffected by the political influences around him. Cook himself recalled that the first stirrings of his political consciousness began, in fact, during the religious revival:

> towards the end of the Revival a certain faculty of scepticism and critical judgement asserted itself in me. I realised that as a popular movement the Revival was an abnormal and aberrant manifestation of the spirit of the Welsh people, and that this powerful current of feeling flowing as strong as a tide produced astonishingly little change in the fundamental economic and industrial facts of the miner's life. It did, indeed, divert the attention of the miners from these facts. And that, as I was beginning to see, was wrong.

From this point onwards Cook took an increasing interest in

trade union matters. It was typical of Arthur Cook that his early involvement expressed itself in the desire to help others. His landlord's front room was converted on Saturday mornings into a miners' consultation office. There Cook helped miners fill in the complicated forms necessary to claim their full wages and compensation entitlements. His career as a leader of men had begun.

Had he come to the Rhondda in an earlier, more torpid, generation, or had he migrated to a more prosperous coalfield such as Nottinghamshire, Arthur Cook may well have remained locked within the ideological confines of nonconformity. Peaceful progress may have assuaged his desire for social improvement. But Cook had come to South Wales in 1901, when economic trends were running against the survival of tranquillity. A complex mixture of causal factors, the most fundamental of which was falling living standards, undermined harmonious industrial relations. Arthur Cook, a young man with an intense interest in the well-being of his fellows, became deeply affected by the social and economic developments within the coalfield. And in the decade after his arrival in Porth these trends moved in a radical direction – falling profitability, declining real wages, decomposition of old political allegiances, and the rise of a new generation of young miners imbued with a passion to overthrow the system of coal ownership with which they identified the hardship, poverty and injustice suffered by the mining communities. By 1919 industrial relations in the coalfield had been poisoned. Arthur Cook's twenties coincided with a dramatic radicalisation of many miners' political outlook. And the Rhondda was the cockpit of this transition.

A detailed account of the factors producing the unique conditions in the South Wales coalfield after 1908 is inappropriate here. They have been studied elsewhere, notably by L. J. Williams in his article 'The Road to Tonypandy'.[3] Suffice to say that the waning influence of religion, the continued trend towards amalgamation of collieries into powerful combines, the impotence of prevailing political representation and, above all, falling living standards, contributed to the rise of a disgruntled, strongly unionised and potentially powerful work-force. The symbolic end-product of this transfiguration was the Cambrian Combine dispute of 1910-11 and the Tonypandy riots which shattered the uneasy peace which had existed between owners and miners in the Rhondda. Partners to that peace, facilitators of it, indeed, had been a moderate SWMF leadership. Men like William Abraham ('Mabon'), President of the SWMF, saw an identity of interest between men and employers which was based on the notion of mutual progress. When economic conditions deteriorated after 1903 this attitude of conservatism and conciliation became increasingly incongruous. Younger men did not share their leaders' over-optimistic faith in peaceful progress. Men like Noah Ablett and Noah Rees, whose very names testified to the devoutness which gripped so many, forsook the chapel and strained on the leash of moderate leadership. Furthermore, they (and especially Ablett) had the intellect and imagination to dream of and plan for a new form of society where 'the slave of the lamp' would wrest control of their own destiny away from the class which exploited them and the form of leadership which perpetuated such injustice. Arthur Cook was part of this generation. Indeed his experience was typical of the ideological shift that took place in the minds of many perceptive young miners.

As the religious revival lost its grip during 1905, Cook became responsive to a more radical social movement. The circumstances surrounding Cook's leap out of nonconformity into socialism are unclear. It is likely that his first formal move towards political activity occured in 1906. An ILP branch had been established in Porth the previous December, and Cook apparently later came

7

into contact with William Trainer, an ILP propagandist sent into the Rhondda on a recruiting mission. According to John Strachey, who knew Cook quite well, Cook joined the ILP soon afterwards and, as he 'did nothing by halves', immediately became an active and outspoken member of his branch. Such political involvement did not sit easily alongside chapel-going. Soon Cook was in trouble with his minister, to whom members of the congregation had complained about Cook's political garrulity. Made to choose between his lifelong allegiance to the chapel and his growing involvement with the union and ILP, Cook resigned from the chapel. It must have been a painful decision, not least due to the effect it must have had on his mother. Annie Cook, who sang in the chapel choir, resigned with her husband.

After this watershed Cook threw himself wholeheartedly into union work. In his own words, Cook became known to the Trefor colliery management as 'one of those agitators'. That same year he moved from the Trefor pit to the nearby Coedcae 'house-coal' colliery, the smallest of the Lewis–Merthyr mines in the Porth district. Once at Coedcae Cook advanced rapidly within the union lodge (Strachey stated that Cook became chairman in 1906 – a sudden elevation which seems hardly credible). Cook himself claimed that before 1914 he had held at various times every official position – chairman, secretary, treasurer and minimum wage and compensation secretary – within the Coedcae lodge. There are no official records to verify this statement, but Cook's name appears in the available minute-books in April 1910 when he was a Coedcae delegate to the Lewis–Merthyr Employees' Joint Committee (LMJC), an organisation which had grown out of the lodges in the Lewis–Merthyr combine so as to mirror union structure with the pattern of coal ownership. Arthur Cook, therefore, was a growing influence within the local echelons of the SWMF at a time when the South Wales miners were emerging from a relatively quiescent period. After 1906 coalfield newspapers reveal a growing anticipation of battle. In 1908 a major dispute at the Powell Duffryn collieries in Aberdare (at the head of the valley next to the Rhondda) shattered the insecure peace. Subsequently a host of small localised altercations proliferated throughout the coalfield. Though physically unconnected, these outbreaks were symptomatic of a general disorder caused by worsening economic conditions. The SWMF leadership reacted to this disturbing development by hiding its collective head in the sand; it condemned strike action and urged men to abide by the conciliation agreements that had been negotiated for them. But conciliation was not working. Perceptive miners like Arthur Cook could recognise the trends running against them: all signposted the need for a major departure from the cautious policies and organisational deficiencies perpetuated by the SWMF leadership. Real wages had been falling since 1903 under the Conciliation Board agreements between the coalowners and the SWMF. In addition, employers were attempting to lower money wages through colliery price lists. At the same time the SWMF, despite persistent non-unionism, was a powerful trade union; many miners felt the Federation was strong enough to force important concessions from the owners. But the conservatism of the SWMF's leadership was endemic: the South Wales miners were confronted with an officialdom ideologically incapable of instituting the aggressive policy necessary to achieve major advances. Furthermore, the sporadic but persistent disputes had, for many rank and file miners, a significance deeper than their immediate cause. As Hywel Francis and Dai Smith have recognised, 'The issue of control, albeit on a small scale and about "work" matters, was at stake; certainly the question of control, in the wider social sense, was in the minds of the most ardent opponents and proponents of the men.'[4] And yet the SWMF was structurally unsuited to the implementation of a militant policy, hampered by its federal nature where each geographical district had a high degree of autonomy and was ruled by its local union boss – or 'Czar' as Tom Richards put it – the miners' agent.

Miners of radical thought in the Rhondda could, then, be clear about certain things: the capitalist structure of the coal industry was based on injustice and exploitation; the way forward (in terms of immediate advances and long-term abolition of private ownership) lay through the use of industrial power; but the SWMF was presently incapable, due to its organisation and leadership, of delivering the goods. Such men searched for ideas and strategies to suit the situation they perceived. And they found them. To understand the development of Arthur Cook's philosophy we must examine the attitudes and concepts that were stimulated by events in the Rhondda before 1914. Most of these ideas were brought into those valleys via the actions of one man, the 'schoolmaster' of the band of young, talented and politically conscious miners – Noah Ablett. Like Cook, Ablett was born in 1883; like Cook he had been a boy preacher. But Ablett's conversion to socialism was quicker, and in 1907 he was chosen to attend Ruskin College, Oxford, on a scholarship from the Rhondda No. 1 District of the SWMF. There Ablett came into contact with the British Advocates of Industrial Unionism, established in 1906 by the Socialist Labour Party in order to prepare the ground for the establishment of revolutionary trade unions in opposition to existing organisations. On his return to South Wales at the end of his studies, Ablett formed a branch of the BAIU in Porth, distributing industrial unionist literature in the area. The proposal to create *new* unions did not, however, attract much support amongst miners who were committed to the SWMF even if they were dissatisfied with its leadership and structure. Ablett soon began to move away from the strict BAIU stance and channelled his energies into the radicalisation and reform of the SWMF. He became an early proponent of 'industrial syndicalism'. This was a British synthesis of American industrial unionism and French anarcho-syndicalism. Both doctrines were based on the belief that the workers could capture control of their own industries by aggressive use of strike action, with a general strike regarded as the ultimate weapon for the overthrow of capitalism. The French doctrine rejected the replacement of existing unions, and encouraged instead the amalgamation, reorganisation and radicalisation of those bodies. These 'industrial unions' were to be the instruments to carry out a militant policy of direct action leading to immediate improvement of conditions and the gradual expropriation of capitalism. Profits would be absorbed and the industries then taken over by the workers. Syndicalism also entailed the rejection of parliamentary action, and this was attractive to many of those British socialists who had become pessimistic about the potential of the House of Commons to deliver the fundamental changes in society they dreamt of.

It is revealing that of the South Wales syndicalists to emerge by 1912 Ablett, Cook, George Dolling, W. H. Mainwaring and others had all been (or still were) members of the ILP. This trend towards syndicalism within the ILP was supplemented from the early months of 1909 by the activities of the Plebs League, which had been founded at Ruskin to promote left-wing education amongst workers. Within weeks Plebs branches had been established in five towns in the coalfield, including Porth and Tonypandy.

Arthur Cook, as an ILP and union activist in Porth, must have encountered Ablett and his ideas, although the extent to which he was an adherent to syndicalism at this stage is difficult to judge. The events of 1910-12, however, were to expose Cook and others to the white heat of bitter industrial conflict and open many minds to the revolutionary philosophy and tactics Noah Ablett had been propounding for many months. The extent to which syndicalism was a factor in the widespread labour disputes of 1910-14 is a matter for debate, but recent research reveals that its influence was limited to a small minority of the workers involved. In the Rhondda, however, this revolutionary doctrine was far more significant. The importance of the Cambrian Combine dispute to the nature and timing of radicalisation amongst Rhondda miners must not be underestimated. The strike and its infamous offshoot, the Tonypandy riots, were vital to the spread of syndicalist ideas. The dispute began over the price list for payment to miners working in 'abnormal places' (where output, and therefore earnings, were hampered by geological difficulties) at one of the pits belonging to Cambrian Collieries Ltd. The owners tried to coerce the seventy men in dispute by locking out the entire colliery work-force of 800 men. In response, the whole of the 12,000 men employed by the Cambrian Combine struck work. The strike was to last almost one year; it produced tension which came to breaking-point with the Tonypandy rioting in November. Thereafter the dispute became a bitter war of attrition which the miners eventually lost. Cook was involved on the periphery of the conflagration, during which he helped to organise the feeding of strikers' children (a typically humanitarian contribution). But the conditions created by the strike seem to have drawn him much closer to Ablett and his growing circle of syndicalists. On 27 May 1911 a group of militants within the SWMF met in Cardiff to discuss questions arising out of the Cambrian Combine struggle. The secretary to this meeting was W. H. Mainwaring, a prominent member of the Cambrian lodge and one of the nub of syndicalists present who were soon to form themselves into the Unofficial Reform Committee (URC). Ablett advocated the widening of the Cambrian dispute, calling for a national front at MFGB conferences to demand a minimum wage throughout the British coalfields. Two days later a further meeting of militants passed a resolution moved by Charlie Gibbons from Maerdy: 'That we form ourselves into a party for the purpose of propagating advanced thought, and that we appoint persons in different sections of the coalfield for the purpose of getting the names of members and for the purpose of correspondence.'[5] Mainwaring's pencilled notes of the first Cardiff meeting mention that a person named Cook took part in the general discussion. Mainwaring, however, stated subsequently that Arthur Cook 'was not known even to any of us at the time'. But this is not so. Charlie Gibbons, the mover of the resolution on 29 May, writing in 1913, recalled how he became involved with the URC group:

> quite by accident I happened to attend a debate at the Lewis–Merthyr lodge room. It was a debate between Noah Ablett and Mardy Jones on the question of the relative merits of the Central Labour College as against Ruskin College ... As a result of that debate I got into touch with Noah Ablett, George Dolling, W. F. Hay and others such as Arthur Cook and Will Mainwaring, and my real education on trade unionism was begun.[6]

This evidence also supplies a clue to the likely area of contact between Cook and the men of 'advanced thought'. In 1909, the Central Labour College (CLC) was founded as a more radical form of workers' education than that offered at Ruskin. Ablett toured the coalfield in an attempt to persuade SWMF districts to subscribe to the CLC. In 1911 the Pontypridd and Rhondda District (known colloquially as Rhondda No. 2) decided to send a student to the CLC, and Arthur Cook was to win the two-year scholarship.

By the end of August 1911 the URC had moved its meetings to Tonypandy, and plans were drawn up the following month for the preparation of a pamphlet expounding the group's programme. In November the URC met in Pontypridd to put the finishing touches to the pamphlet, which they named *The Miners' Next Step*. The following month it was sent to the printers. The question of who actually wrote this famous booklet has caused some controversy. Cook claimed that he was part-author along with Ablett, Mainwaring and Hay. Mainwaring's minutes of URC meetings do not mention Cook in this respect, however, and Francis and Smith (the recent historians of the SWMF) have concluded that Cook made no contribution to the publication. The issue is complicated by the fact that Mainwaring's record of authorship does not account for the first two chapters of the pamphlet. The evidence, while not conclusive, suggests that while Cook had opportunities to debate early drafts of the work, make suggestions and propose alterations, he cannot be termed one of its authors. It is interesting to note, however, that in subsequent years the capitalist press, coalowners and governments made great play of Cook's 'authorship' in attempts to discredit him, and yet he never denied responsibility. Perhaps this was because the ideas and policies contained in *The Miners' Next Step* matched Cook's own ideas so neatly.

The Miners' Next Step caused a furore amongst workers, coalowners and press. The pamphlet has received welcome attention in recent years from historians and publishers; it is sufficient here, therefore, to note some of its more salient points, made all the more pertinent because they provide a direct line to an understanding of Cook's philosophy. The pamphlet opened with a critique of conciliation and the autocratic leadership it demanded. In order to destroy this form of leadership, rank and file control of the union was demanded. The authors urged the formation of an industrial union (the establishment of a centralised South Wales miners' union was to be a major step in this direction) capable of paralysing the mining industry when taking strike action. Sympathetic action with other unions and a policy striving persistently to obtain the best possible conditions were also demanded. The 'Programme' included a phrase which highlighted of the pamphlet's rationale: 'the suggested organization is constructed to fight rather than negotiate. It is based on the principle that we can only get what we are strong enough to win and retain.' In place of conciliation, the authors demanded that 'the old policy of identity of interest between employers and ourselves be abolished and a policy of open hostility installed'. The pamphlet rejected nationalisation and advocated instead a system of workers' ownership achieved by a policy of 'encroaching control':

> a continual agitation be carried on in favour of increasing the minimum wage and shortening the hours of work, until we have extracted the whole of the employers' profit . . . our objective (is) to build up an organization that will ultimately take over the mining industry and carry it on in the interests of the workers.

Arthur Cook may not have been an author of *The Miners' Next Step,* but this is almost irrelevant. The pamphlet's insistence 'that we can only get what we are strong enough to win and retain' underpinned his leadership henceforth. Similarly, the booklet's recognition of the class struggle, its advocacy of an industrial union, its plea for rank and file control of the union, and the need to form alliances with other unions, were to remain central to Cook's ideology and strategy. Time and change were to undermine Cook's adherence to the pamphlet's rejection of parliamentary action; the economic calamities and industrial defeats which the miners were to suffer in the 1920s made the syndicalist policy of 'the mines for the miners' impracticable; but deep down Arthur Cook was to remain a syndicalist.

Throughout 1910 and 1911 Cook consolidated his position within the Coedcae lodge and the LMJC. He was chosen frequently to attend deputations to the pit management, to address miners' meetings and present discussion papers. In October 1911, however, at the height of the seminal period within the Rhondda syndicalist movement, Cook left Porth to begin his studies at the CLC in Earls Court, London. The CLC was founded to provide education based on the recognition of the antagonism between capital and labour, and sought to arouse working-class awareness of this conflict. One of the CLC's prime functions was to train students to be both militant leaders and teachers. To this end lectures were given in sociology, logic, rhetoric, English language, elementary science, social movements, industrial history, and economics. All subjects were taught from a Marxist viewpoint. From this point onwards Cook was a self-avowed Marxist. His reading at Earls Court would have included *Capital, The Communist Manifesto, Wage, Labour and Capital,* and other books written by Marx and Engels. Cook reached the age of twenty-eight shortly after the start of the course, and in view of this maturity and his later garrulity one may have expected him to make a big impact at the college. In fact, he does not appear to have been as prominent in CLC circles as, for example, Charlie Gibbons (at the college on a Rhondda No, 1 District scholarship). Cook took his turn to chair house meetings, but from November 1911 to March 1912 he made only small contributions to student debates. In March the CLC students held a debate on whether 'in the opinion of this house political action is essential to the interests of the working class'. Cook presented the case for the negative (he lost by fourteen votes to thirty one).

The national miners' strike proved a frustrating experience for the South Wales militants. They had begun so successfully, when their agitation for a minimum wage permeated the British coalfields and became immediate MFGB policy. Following the coalowners' refusal to concede the demand, the first ever national coal strike was called. The strike was solid, the men quietly resolute and confident of victory. The MFGB leadership, however, were eager to compromise and accepted a government Minimum Wage Bill lacking definition of actual minimum wage figures. A return to work followed a ballot vote of the men which failed to produce a two-thirds majority in favour of staying out.

The South Wales miners, in fact, voted against continuation of the strike. A combination of strike-weariness following the Cambrian and other sectional stoppages, added to the depletion of financial reserves (both union and personal), produced such a vote. This was a damaging blow to the URC, which responded with bitter criticism of the MFGB and SWMF leadership. Towards the end of 1911 the *Rhondda Socialist* newspaper had been launched. Colloquially known as 'the Workers' Bomb', the paper expressed a wide range of opinions, but the syndicalist viewpoint gained prominence within its columns. At the termination of the coal strike W. F. Hay, writing under the cryptic pseudonym of 'Syndic', warned the SWMF leadership: 'A bitter day of reckoning is coming for those who, like Hartshorn, Brace, Richards, Onions, etc., have seized upon, misled and betrayed the most important industrial movement of modern times.' In June the syndicalists launched an attempt to reorganise the SWMF on the lines suggested in *The Miners' Next Step*. Despite obtaining support from the Federation conference delegates, the move was blocked by the SWMF leadership. Undismayed, the syndicalists continued to propagate their ideas: in August 1912 the Rhondda Socialist Society (RSS) was founded, reflecting the ideological groupings expressed in the columns of the 'Workers' Bomb' (ie, there was domination by the URC). That same month Arthur Cook returned to Porth for the CLC's summer vacation. The *Rhondda Socialist* reported that

> Messrs. Charles L. Gibbons (Maerdy), Arthur Cook (Porth), and W. Nefydd Thomas (Penycraig), the three Rhondda Miners' Federation students at the Central Labour College, are now in the districts. The Plebs Club and Institute, Tonypandy, has been favoured with excellent addresses from the three Comrades, and those who heard their addresses testify to the splendid progress made by them during their stay at the Central Labour College.

Nefydd Thomas returned to Earls Court in October, and Charlie

Gibbons was sent by the CLC to the Manchester District to teach local classes. Arthur Cook, however, remained in Porth. Cook stated that the Coedcae colliery management revoked their promise to keep his job for him, and he was therefore forced to return to the coal-face a year earlier than anticipated. Cook put his experience at the CLC to immediate use, becoming involved in the development of local classes held under the college's auspices. In September 1912 he organised an economics class in Porth, with Hay as lecturer. The following month Cook addressed the Pontypridd Trades and Labour Council on the subject 'Education and the Working Class'. Opposing university education, he spoke in favour of the CLC's teaching: 'Knowledge is power, but power for whom: the boss or the worker? An education which will benefit the working class is one which will give them a clear insight into the system of wealth production and distribution, for the purpose of abolishing wage slavery.'[7] In March 1913 Cook arranged for Dennis Hird, the Principal of the CLC, to address a meeting of the same organisation, and Cook himself spoke to a branch meeting of railwaymen on the benefits of the CLC.

Cook also played a leading role in the syndicalists' next venture, the formation of the Industrial Democracy League (IDL). The IDL was intended as an expansion of the URC, incorporating rank and file organisations in other South Wales trades. The URC sought to dispel any appearance of industrial parochialism, and to follow up *The Miners' Next Step's* goal of alliances of unions. In March 1913 the IDL published a manifesto 'to Militant Trade Unions in South Wales', in which many points from *The Miners' Next Step* were reiterated, and which called for an overhaul of trade union organisation:

> renovate it, transform it, shape it into a weapon to wrest control of industry from the capitalist, later to afford a medium for adminis-

trating the industry by the workers themselves... one industry cannot stand by itself alone ... we must link up industries with Industrial Unionism, both for offence and defence... until we make the defeat of Labour in any struggle a sheer impossibility.

It was an aim of Arthur Cook's leadership throughout his life.

Following his return to Port in August 1912 it took little time for Cook to regain his official position within the Coedcae lodge. By January 1913 he was once more a delegate to the LMJC. Throughout that year he made rapid progress within the Joint Committee, becoming a leading participant in deputations and meetings. By the end of 1913 he was chairman of the Coedcae lodge, and his impact within the local union structure was confirmed in January 1914 when he was elected chairman of the LMJC. This was a position of great importance and responsibility, and yet we must not forget that Cook was only just past his thirtieth birthday. He also made progress within the ranks of the local syndicalist and CLC movement. In June 1913 the *South Wales Worker* (successor to the *Rhondda Socialist*) announced that Cook had been appointed secretary of the Porth branch of the IDL. He strengthened his credibility as a syndicalist by resigning from the ILP. By October 1913 Cook had been appointed Honorary Secretary of the General Committee of the Rhondda District Branch of the CLC and, with Ablett, Hay and Nefydd Thomas, formed its staff of lecturers. His commitment to the CLC was emphasised in July 1914 when he moved the resolution at a SWMF conference calling for the take-over of the CLC by the Federation and National Union of Railwaymen – a proposal that was implemented two years later.

While Cook and the syndicalists were trying to expand their influence, however, rank and file support for their policies was waning. In the aftermath of the national strike, and with a boom in production, militant activity slumped. By the end of 1913 the

IDL had contracted to the verge of extinction. In July 1914 Cook commented that a SWMF conference that month 'was one of the tamest I have ever attended, the revolutionary spirit lying dormant'. And within a few weeks the last vestiges of militancy were to be submerged by the sea of patriotic fervour that engulfed the coalfield.

By the outbreak of the Great War Arthur Cook had become a trade union leader of importance, the chairman of a Joint Committee representing some ten thousand miners. A working miner himself still, Cook was a revolutionary and a teacher of revolutionary ideas; he was a husband and a father, and yet after his shift underground he must have spent most of his time in meetings and classes (and he taught a weekly CLC in Barry, twenty miles from Porth!). Despite the radicalisation of the South Wales miners in these pre-war years, it is obvious that Cook's rise in the union owed a great deal to men who did not share his extreme views; and it is likely that even a non-socialist miner would have found it difficult to question Cook's work-rate and dedication. Since his decision to put union and political work before religion in 1906 Cook had come a long way in a short time. But the outbreak of war posed questions for Cook and the militants in the Rhondda; the importance of South Wales coal to the war effort placed union officials in positions of enhanced responsibility. Would such power curb Cook's commitment to an aggressive industrial policy? How would this emerging leader of the Left, whose own father had been a career soldier, respond to the enormity of war conditions?

2 'An agitator of the worst type'

When the First World War broke out those in Britain who voiced protest were few and silenced quickly. Anyone who stood up to condemn the country's involvement was unlikely to be standing for long. The sheer weight and vigour of the pro-war response among rank and file miners threw the militants into disarray. In the autumn of 1913 Arthur Cook had written articles for the *South Wales Worker* in which he criticised the build-up of the armed forces and prophesied compulsory military service. But in the late summer and autumn of 1914 Cook does not appear to have openly condemned British participation. In fact the URC element within the coalfield made a weak response to the war. Of the Rhondda syndicalists only W. F. Hay made an early and clear statement of opposition to war, 'the sport of kings, the hired assassins' trade'.[1] Noah Ablett remained silent on the issue until 1917; Charlie Gibbons joined the Royal Army Medical Corps in the autumn of 1914. Some militants on the fringes of the URC, like Frank Hodges and George Barker, were publicly pro-war and urged recruitment into the armed forces.

Arthur Cook certainly did not make patriotic/jingoist speeches or encourage Porth miners to enlist. In fact his activities in the early months of the war were concerned with mitigating the adverse effects of the conflict on those at home. On 9 August Cook and Gibbons planned to hold a public meeting to protest against increases in food prices; the meeting, however, was banned by the Deputy Chief Constable – an early indication of the political role the police were to play during the war. By October Cook was the leading figure in the Porth Relief Committee, established to deal with hardship amongst the community. Writing in the *Porth Gazette,* Cook showed his concern for the welfare of soldiers' families and made clear his disgust with the government's sense of priorities:

> While enthusiasm is being risen on behalf of recruiting, the dependents of those serving the colours are being forgotten. The price paid for the patriotism of our men leaving wives and children behind, enables their loved ones to live on a bread and dripping diet. Of such in England's honour. . .
>
> Why should the wives and dependents of our soldiers and sailors depend on charity? Why should wages be taxed? Is there not sufficient wealth in this country to provide handsomely for these people? . . . The cost of living is increasing. Let us rouse the conscience of the British public to force the Government to take over their responsibilities. . .
>
> Seeing the wives and children are deprived of their rightful defenders and can make no organised protest we must do our duty as trade unionists and as citizens to force the Government, who in one night could vote £100 millions for destruction of human life to see that justice is meted out to these unfortunates. Remember our first duty is to those at home.[2]

One has to read between the lines to detect Cook's opposition to the war, but once again his basic humanitarianism is apparent.

Coinciding with the outbreak of war, Cook had his own problems which may have disturbed the clarity of his response to international events. He had moved from Coedcae to the Hafod pit, a much larger Lewis–Merthyr colliery nearby, earlier in 1914; in August the Hafod management gave him the sack and fourteen days' notice to quit the company house he rented. This was seen as blatant victimisation by the local union lodges. On 14 August a special meeting of the LMJC heard the Hafod delegates report Cook's case, and the following day a mass meeting of the Lewis–Merthyr miners unanimously resolved to ask the company to withdraw their notices. The management refused, and the next mass meeting threatened strike action to protect Cook who 'has proven himself a very active member of his trade union'. This threat persuaded the Lewis–Merthyr company to abort their attempt to dismiss Cook; obviously they had been surprised by Cook's popularity amongst the workmen and by the solidarity of the local union.

With his job at the Hafod colliery secured, Cook's attention could be focused fully on conditions affecting his members and their families. The MFGB refused to be a party to the Treasury Agreement of March 1915, whereby most trade union leaders abrogated their members' right to strike as part of an industrial truce. Nevertheless, the MFGB officials were keen to safeguard both an adequate supply of coal to the navy and an adequate supply of miners to the trenches; the national Federation was partner to a tacit no-strike agreement, while its leaders became unofficial recruiting officers. As the winter of 1914-15 wore on, however, this 'truce' was subject to increasing strain. The root cause, undoubtedly, was the soaring cost of living. In mining areas discontent was exacerbated by the knowledge that while inflation eroded living standards, coalowners were making huge profits from high coal prices. In March 1915 the MFGB demanded a twenty per cent wage increase to compensate for inflation. The coalowners refused to discuss a national wage rise, and negotiations reverted to the districts. Agreements were arrived at satisfactorily in most areas, but in South Wales the owners were only prepared to offer ten per cent. The SWMF pressed for a national strike and, when that was refused, struck alone in July 1915. Because of the importance of Welsh steam coal to the navy, the government intervened quickly, and was forced to concede an eighteen-and-a-half per cent wage increase. Speaking at a MFGB conference five years later, Arthur Cook declared that the 1915 strike had 'made'· the SWMF, and indeed the flagging vitality of the militants was revived. As Martin Woodhouse revealed, 'the pre-war URC were brought back into circulation and former leaders of the URC made a re-appearance on a syndicalist platform.'[3] Cook was prominent in this rejuvenation. At a meeting of the URC in Tonypandy on 5 August Cook was delegated, along with Ablett, Mainwaring and B. R. Pryce, to draw up a manifesto on proposals for the reorganisation of the SWMF. A further meeting later that month saw Cook take the chair. The ranks of the URC had been thinned, no doubt, by the impact of war, but it is interesting to note Cook's prominence within the syndicalist group in 1915.

The URC's interest in union reform appears to have been short-lived; the anti-war movement, however, began to grow, spurred on by the fear of compulsory national service which developed in proportion to the slaughter in the fields of Europe. The SWMF actually voted in favour of taking strike action if conscription was introduced. It was not necessary to be against the war to oppose conscription, but the response of the South Wales militants was consciously and explicitly anti-war. In April 1916 Cook made his opposition to the war unequivocally apparent, although he advocated intensification of industrial struggle rather than a political campaign by the SWMF against continued fighting:

> Daily I see signs amongst the working class with whom I move and work of a mighty awakening. The chloroforming pill of patriotism is failing in its power to drug the mind and consciousness of the worker. He is beginning to shudder at his stupidity in allowing himself to become a party to such a catastrophe as we see today. The chains of slavery are being welded tighter upon us than ever. The ruling classes are over-reaching themselves in their hurry to enslave us . . . Economic conditions are forcing the workers to think; the scales are falling from their eyes. Men are wanted to give a lead. Comrades I appeal to you to rouse your union to protect the liberties

of its members. An industrial truce was entered into by our leaders behind our backs which had opened the way for any encroachment upon our rights and liberties. Away with the industrial truce! We must not stand by and allow the workers to be exploited and our liberties taken away.[4]

Cook's unwillingness to sanction the surrender of 'rights and liberties' for the sake of the war effort became more vocal. By mid-1916 the drain of miners into the armed forces was seriously affecting coal output. In a memorandum to the War Cabinet the Foreign Office claimed that if another fifteen-and-a-half million tons of coal per year were not forthcoming, the Allies' fighting capacity would be hampered, and requested the implementation of measures to limit absenteeism in the pits. Within the month attempts were made to establish Absentee Committees at the collieries, with the MFGB's and SWMF's approval. But many miners' lodges refused to form such committees. A mass meeting of Lewis–Merthyr men on 9 July decided not to participate. Cook almost certainly played an important part in that decision.

Before 1917 Cook was not part of any concerted anti-war campaign, but he became a lightning rod for the growing dissatisfaction amongst Lewis–Merthyr miners. High prices were a constant source of unrest; resentment grew as living standards fell, and agitation was soon under way for a further substantial wage increase and the removal of income tax from the men's wages. On 9 November 1916 the Lewis–Merthyr miners, with Cook as chairman, and Noah Ablett the other main speaker, passed resolutions against income tax and in support of the SWMF's demand for a fifteen-per-cent wage increase. Despite their massive profits the South Wales coalowners refused to grant an increase; a strike was imminent when the government stepped in to impose state control of the coalfield and agree a wage rise. For Arthur Cook this was another sign of the miners' industrial strength and, true to his philosophy, it encouraged him to press for even better wages and conditions. He was involved in a multitude of small disputes between the men and management at the Lewis–Merthyr collieries. Invariably he urged aggressive action. From November 1916 onwards his activities attracted the attention of the local police and Home Office intelligence. The Home Office papers chart many of his public actions during the last three years of the war. The police engaged shorthand writers and plain-clothes officers to record his meetings, and the reports show Cook's emergence as an anti-war leader as well as his militant industrial involvement. The documents are a remarkable record, both of Cook's activities and the workings of police and government surveillance. In January 1917 Cook's energetic and militant leadership of the Lewis–Merthyr men was rewarded by his re-election as LMJC chairman. Immediately afterwards Cook was at the forefront of another confrontation. The massive casualties on the battlefields of Europe prompted the government to draft men from essential industries who had hitherto been exempt from conscription; 20,000 miners were to be 'combed out' of the pits and into the army. The SWMF leaders reluctantly agreed to this, but opposition at rank and file level was vociferous. The Lewis–Merthyr men began to defy the military recruiting authorities. On 28 January 1917 a mass meeting protested at the decision to withdraw exemption certificates from practically half the surfaceworkers and many underground men at the Bertie and Trefor collieries. The following month the LMJC resolved to 'resist the comb-out by every means in our power even to laying down tools'. Not surprisingly, Cook was the prime mover in this protest, and he took steps to obstruct the military's attempts to recruit men – he posted notices at the local collieries advising miners to disobey instructions to report for army examination.

Such behaviour brought Cook to the attention of the Chief Constable of Glamorgan, Capt. Lionel Lindsay who, from 1917 onwards, was preoccupied – one might even use the word obsessed – with the emergence of an anti-war movement within the ranks of the South Wales militants. Following Cook's defiance of the recruiting authorities Lindsay pressed the Home Office for permission to prosecute, but was turned down. Cook, no doubt unaware of Lindsay's urge to put him behind bars, grew even bolder in his public utterances:

> I am no pacifist when war is necessary to free my class from the curse and enslavement of capitalism. . . What, then, is my opposition to the 'Comb-out'? . . . As a worker I have more regard for the interests of my class than any nation. The interests of my class are not benefitted by this war, hence my opposition. Comrades, let us take heart, there are thousands of miners in Wales who are prepared to fight for their class. War against war must be the workers' cry.[5]

It is evident that by early 1917 increasing war-weariness, conscription and industrial discontent had prompted the growth of an anti-war ambience in the South Wales coalfield. From March onwards, however, this sentiment developed into a mass movement. The Russian Revolution of February 1917 was of fundamental importance to this transformation. For the growing anti-war minority the overthrow of the Romanovs was seen not only as the emanciption of Russian workers but also as an opportunity for a rapid end to hostilities. Advanced elements within the South Wales labour movement were quick to adopt this latter position. On 15 April 1917 a mass meeting of Lewis-Merthyr men, chaired by Cook, called for a SWMF conference 'to get a resolution passed in favour of peace by negotiations'. The post-February anti-war movement in South Wales has been ably researched by David Egan;[6] he has shown that events in Russia were only partially understood, but the peace formula of 'no annexations, no indemnities' that emanated from it was seized upon as a blueprint for a negotiated end to hostilities. The Russian Revolution thus shone as a beacon for the anti-war element in the coalfield. In June Cook and other Rhondda militants attended the Leeds Convention summoned to welcome the Revolution and to support the foreign policy of the Russian Provisional Government. On 2 July Cook was involved in meetings at Ynyshir and Porth (where he was chairman) where resolutions were passed demanding 'an immediate conference of the belligerents to negotiate an immediate cessation of hostilities on the lines of the Russian Manifesto, of no annexations, no indemnities'. Cook told the meetings:

> Since the day of the declaration of war I have unflinchingly opposed the same. To hell with everybody bar my class. To me, the hand of the German and Austrian is the same as the hand of my fellow-workmen at home. I am an internationalist. Russia has taken the step, and it is due to Britain to second the same and secure peace and leave the war and its cost to the capitalist who made it for the profiteer.[7]

Cook's 'unflinching opposition' was not so evident at the outset of the war, but the confidence with which militants had now taken an anti-war position was evidence of growing mass support for their policies. And Cook in 1917 was prepared to condemn the war from an explicitly Marxist viewpoint.

The rapid growth of the anti-war element was accompanied by a revival of the URC as part of a bona fide revolutionary movement. The URC was active throughout the first half of 1917 in promoting opposition to the 'comb-out'. Furthermore, Cook was deeply involved in the upsurge of the local CLC network which took place in unison with the renewed potency of the syndicalists. In March 1917 there were nineteen CLC classes in South Wales; by December there were forty-one. Cook taught three of these – economics at Ynyshir, and industrial history and economics at Ynysybwl and Taffs Well. These did not escape the attention of the local police – Deputy Chief Constable John Williams informed his superior officer that 'he (Cook) lectures at so-called "Economics Classes" where it is impossible to over-hear his words, and I am satisfied that he carries on an insidious campaign against law and order'.[8] Cook's reputation was begin-ning to grow, and it is interesting that even the non-socialist *Porth Gazette* was prepared to commend him: 'In our opinion Mr Cook is one of the real hopes of the Labour Movement. A young man full of real enthusiasm and divine indignation at the condition of the masses. If he were not quite so enthusiastic Mr Cook would take nore time, avoid repeating himself and make a very good speaker'.[9] Less welcome attention was being paid by the constabulary, however, and from October 1918 a new source of surveillance was introduced with the launch of an intelligence section within the Ministry of Labour. Cook played a leading part in the URC's campaign against the 'comb-out'. He made a verbal attack on General Smuts, who had been sent by the Cabinet into South Wales to encourage resistance to syndicalist and pacifist influence. At a meeting on the mountainside at Hafod on 28 October Cook tried to stir up opposition to Smuts's visit to Tonypandy the following day. Within a few weeks Capt. Lindsay was baying for Cook's imprisonment:

> It was only reported to me by a Recruiting Officer last night that A. J. Cook, the agitator from the Lewis–Merthyr Colliery, Trehafod, Glamorgan, who I have frequently reported for disloyal utterances, without success, openly declared, whilst denouncing the Recruiting Authorities at Pontypridd, that if he decided that a man should not join the Army the Military Authorities would not dare to send him. . .
>
> Anyone with the slightest knowldede of human nature must be well aware that to punish a conceited upstart of this type, especially when he is a man of no real influence, like Cook, always gives universal satisfaction.[10]

In December Lindsay urged the military authorities in Cardiff to sanction the prosecution of Cook, George Dolling and Arthur Horner from Ynyshir. In January 1918, he brought another case against 'the notorious Arthur J. Cook' to the Commanding Officer, pleading that 'To continue to refrain from punishing this notorious sedition-monger is, to my mind, criminal, and is bound to result in painful revelations later.' And Cook's anti-war message got bolder. At a meeting in Ynyshir on 20 January 1918 he proclaimed:

> Are we going to allow this war to go on? The government wants a hundred thousand men. They demand fifty thousand immediately, and the Clyde workers would not allow the government to take them. Let us stand by them, and show them that Wales will do the same. I have two brothers in the army who were forced to join, but I say "No!" I will be shot before I go to fight. Are you going to allow us to be taken to the war? If so, I say there will not be a ton of coal for the navy.

Towards the end of 1917 Cook began touring the Rhondda, conducting a series of debates on the question of whether food should be rationed. His companion in the debates was George Dolling, one of the authors of *The Miners' Next Step*. Following the Bolshevik seizure of power in November 1917 it seems the Cook-Dolling debates were surreptitious outlets for revolutionary propaganda. In the course of one debate Cook was said to have recommended a revoution, and that 'now is the time for it'. Armed with this evidence, Capt. Lindsay pressed for the prosecution of Cook under the Defence of the Realm Act. His deputy, John Williams, informed the Home Office that Cook 'is an agitator of the worst type and he has been the cause of the major portion of the labour unrest in this district since 1913'. Williams ended his letter by recommending that Cook be tried by court martial, 'even if it is necessary to call him to the Colours so that he can become amenable to Military Law'. Percy Ward, the manager of the Lewis–Merthyr Company, supplied the police and Home Office with valuable information regarding his famous employee and those of his ilk:

> As promised I enclose a list of the ILP and advanced Syndicalists employed at our collieries, who are really the cause of a good deal of the trouble in this part of the coalfield, not only at our own collieries, but also in the neighbourhood. Of this lot, Cook is by far the most dangerous. As he considers himself an orator he has most to say at the various meetings in the district, and without exception, the policy which he preaches is the down-tool policy, and he is also concerned with the peace-cranks.

In March 1918 the Home Office acceded to Lindsay's pressure and Cook was charged on six counts under DORA. His accomplice George Dolling was charged on four counts under the same act. The Home Office had been reluctant to authorise prosecution because of their fear that it would spark off 'a series of strikes and disturbances (that) would mean disaster'. The fears were justified. A mass meeting of miners from the Lewis–Merthyr combine, Ynyshir and Cymmer resolved to strike if the summonses were not annulled. The officials of the Rhondda No. 1 District planned a visit to see the Home Secretary, Sir George Cave, but he would not see them; the prosecutions went ahead. On Wednesday 17 April the Pontypridd Police court was crowded with socialists (including the leading British syndicalist, Tom Mann) and police (including Lindsay and Williams), to witness the trial of Cook and Dolling. In evidence, Cook admitted he had stated the war was the root of evil, but denied that the revolution he had in mind was to be violent. In cross-examination Cook stated the intended revolution was the confiscation of private ownership in food commodities, achieved 'by argument'. He wanted the Triple Alliance of miners, railwaymen and transport workers to use a general strike to persuade the government.

Cook's attitude did not please the Stipendiary. He was found guilty of making statements likely to cause disaffection to His Majesty among the civilian population, and was sentenced to three months' imprisonment. Dolling, who apparently used innuendo rather than direct statement, was acquitted.

A meeting of delegates from lodges throughout the Rhondda Fach and beyond decided to call an immediate strike and to spread it as far as possible. The response to the call was patchy, however, as one could expect for such a narrow issue; on 30 April the strike was called off. The Executive of the SWMF wrote to the Home Secretary protesting about the severity of Cook's sentence, but were informed that there would be no remission. Cook in fact served just two months in prison, and was back in the chair of the LMJC by July.

Wars often accelerate change, and certainly the First World War was an important factor in the rapid rise of Arthur Cook within the South Wales labour movement. This was due largely to the wave of militancy amongst the rank and file miners; Cook's personal advancement came on the crest of this wave. There is no doubt, too, that Cook's imprisonment had a silver lining: he emerged a hero to many, a man who had gone to jail for his beliefs. His friend Arthur Horner, in 1918 a young miners' leader in Maerdy, recalled that by the end of the year Cook 'was beginning to build up a reputation as a leader of the left'. An editorial article in the *Porth Gazette* of April 1919 gives us a clear view of the qualities which earned Cook growing support:

> He had the inspiring personality and the almost fanatical zeal of the true reformer. His character is beyond reproach and his straighforwardness is unquestionable. He may set his goals very far ahead, but he is making for something and he's certainly getting on. And let his biggest opponents not refuse him justice. He is not working for himself; he is not lining his own pocket; all the appearances are

against the accusation of personal ambition; no, the secret of. . . Cook's success is his devotion to the workers, or what he call 'his class'.

Certainly the months ahead saw Cook enter the limelight as the leading figure on the left of the SWMF, a revolutionary who was excited by the opportunities and potential in these post-war years.

Throughout the summer of 1918 the war moved towards an Allied victory. Consequently the anti-war movement lost momentum; but it gave way to the spread of revolutionary ideas. In South Wales, the URC flourished. As early as April 1918 the syndicalists mounted a campaign (which in view of their anti-parliamentarian attitude can only be regarded as a publicity exercise) in the nomination ballot for the SWMF candidate in the vacant parliamentary constituency of East Rhondda. It is interesting that Cook was chosen as an URC representative (he polled 1,816 votes), but puzzling that he was joined by W. H. Mainwaring (1,321 votes), thus splitting the support for the URC. It is quite possible that Mainwaring, who went on to win the seat for Labour in 1933, had already abandoned that anti-parliamentarian position of the syndicalists; his candidature may have been a serious attempt to secure selection. In any event the eventual winner, David Watts Morgan, polled 4,559 votes. In November the Home Office's fortnightly Reports on Revolutionary Organisations in the UK observed that 'since the tremendous events of a week ago (the armistice), the pacifists have been busy tearing off their disguise, and re-appearing in their proper garb as revolutionaries'.

The syndicalists were in the vanguard of a general militancy amongst the miners. The war and state control had a major impact on miners' aspirations. The MFGB's demand for nationalisation had become a matter for immediate consideration: for the miners, more than any other group of workers, continued freedom from governance by the owners was a fundamental objective,

and wartime control had given the MFGB's demand for nationalisation an important boost. William Brace, the moderate Welsh
miners' leader, speaking in October 1919, was of the opinion
that 'The war has driven us at least twenty-five years in advance
of where we were in thought in 1914.' Government control was
accompanied by national wage determination based on pooled
profits – an arrangement which ignored the geological and
economic differences between the various coalfields, and con-
founded the coalowners' traditional contention that national wage
bargaining was impossible. The 'pooled profits' method had some
proximity to nationalisation, and strengthened the importance
of the MFGB as a national negotiating body. It was a point
recognised by both the workers and the coalowners.

Furthermore, the importance of coal to the war effort and
post-war reconstruction gave miners great confidence in their
bargaining power, a belief that an aggressive industrial policy
would reap rich rewards. The South Wales miners displayed an
advanced degree of such confidence. In May 1920, for example,
the government's intelligence survey of revolutionary organisations received the news from one of its regional observers that

> the great mass of workers in South Wales are calmly and confidently
> waiting for some great change that they feel cannot be long delayed.
> I do not wish to be understood as meaning that South Wales is on
> the verge of revolution, or is taking active steps to prepare a revolu-
> tion. What I mean is that the workers of South Wales feel themselves
> absolutely masters of the situation.[11]

The existence of such conviction helps to explain the ambitious
nature of the MFGB's post-war demands presented in January
1919 – a thirty-per-cent wage claim, a reduction of the working
day to six hours, and nationalisation of the mines with joint
control by the workers and state. The MFGB membership voted
in favour of strike action to support these demands by 615,164

to 105,082.

Meanwhile the revolutionary elements within the South Wales coalfield strove for coherence and unity. Attempts were made to revive the old Rhondda Socialist Society, but with a grander title – the South Wales Socialist Society (SWSS). Cook was a leading figure in this initiative, and regarded the SWSS as a sounding-board for the syndicalist/URC programme, eschewing parliamentary activity. According to this viewpoint the 'political socialists' of the ILP, BSP and SLP were subservient to the 'industrial socialists'. Speaking at the inaugural conference of the SWSS, Cook announced that 'The Society was open to all who accepted the class war theory and the Society was to be composed of groups of trades which would consider their own problems and receive the co-operation of the whole in bringing about reforms in their own industries.' He was challenged by Aneurin Bevan, a young militant who had rejected the anti-political nature of syndicalism, and who claimed that the real aim of the URC appeared to be the removal of political organisations as obstructions. He was probably right. Nevertheless, the formation of the SWSS proceeded despite the ideological schism between the syndicalists and the political socialists; but it was to prove a fatal division for the Society. This small episode is important to our understanding of the emergence of Cook's ideas: in 1919 he was still wedded firmly to the anti-political stance of pre-war years; he remained a strict syndicalist.

The URC, meanwhile, kept a comparatively low profile during the MFGB campaign for nationalisation and large improvements in wages and hours. Naturally enough the URC functioned best in times of rank and file discontent, but miners were happy with the MFGB's policies and leadership when wage increases were being achieved easily and when nationalisation appeared a probability rather than the dream it had seemed in pre-war days. Such conditions were infertile soil for the acceptance of URC

35

propaganda, and in June 1919 – when the miners were confident of achieving nationalisation – URC candidates were routed in the SWMF's official elections. Cook, for example, despite his growing reputation, gained only twenty-four conference votes in opposition to James Winstone's 227 in the vice-presidential election.

With hindsight we know that the leadership of the MFGB was outmanoeuvred by Lloyd George, settling for the offer of a Royal Commission rather than pressing for more tangible concessions. The momentum of the MFGB's campaign was halted. The government had decided privately against nationalisation as early as March, but delayed a public announcement until mid-August. The miners, who had been confident that the Royal Commission's condemnation of private ownership would be endorsed by the Cabinet, were shocked and bitter.

These months in 1919 were momentous for the mining communities, and they also witnessed important events in the life of Arthur Cook. The first development, which turned out to be a brief digression, came in March when Cook was nominated by local miners' lodges for election to the Rhondda District Council. Cook was successful and made a sensational impact on the previously staid proceedings of the council chamber. At his first meeting, for example, he spat his condemnation of proposals to hold a peace celebration:

> He was surprised that anyone should want to celebrate peace when there was no peace – and when armies of occupation were in Ireland and India 'crushing our comrades'. The present Paris conference was a war conference sowing the seeds of a future class war. He would welcome a peace which demonstrated the brotherhood of man.

Cook's contentiousness proved a godsend to the local press, who reported with relish his traumatic clashes with fellow-councillors of all political colours. But Cook also worked hard, particularly on matters concerning education and housing improvements. The *Porth Gazette* was once again moved to commend the local firebrand, observing that

> Apart from the occasional outburst of quite uncalled-for and futile belligerency Councillor Cook is co-operating with his fellow townsmen with an aptitude for councillorship which most people did not give him credit for. If he perseveres Mr Cook will yet become as valuable an asset to his township as he undoubtedly is to the workmen he so boldly leads.

Also during the early months of 1919 Cook became involved in events which were to have a much more significant effect on his career. In February 1919, due to the resignation of David Watts Morgan following his election to parliament, the Rhondda No. 1 District of the SWMF decided to appoint a second miners' agent to their staff. In June the District decided that all members of the SWMF were to be eligible for the position. There were twenty-eight applicants, which the District Committee cut to the seventeen who came from the Rhondda No. 1 and Pontypridd and Rhondda Districts. Arthur Cook was one of the candidates. The balloting, according to the exhaustive vote system, began in September. Coincidentally, the temper of the Rhondda miners had been sharpened by Lloyd George's rejection of nationalisation. Militant candidates fared well in the miners' agent election: in the first ballot Cook came a close second to Noah Rees, leader of the Cambrian Combine strike and part-author of *The Miners' Next Step*. In subsequent ballots, however, Cook consistently though narrowly topped the poll, defeating Rees in the final vote by 18,230 to 17,531. This was a remarkable success because most of the Lewis–Merthyr men, as members of the Pontypridd and Rhondda District, could not vote. Cook's success was a testimony to his record of devoted union work and his growing reputation as CLC lecturer, district councillor and militant.

At the beginning of 1920 Cook left the coal-face where he had worked since arriving in the Rhondda. On 4 December 1919 the LMJC – on which Cook had served since 1910, and as chairman since 1914 – congratulated him upon his election. The local paper voiced its rather austere praise:

> We hope Mr Cook will make an able and efficient Agent. He has youth, virility, strong convictions, and a good deal of push. Originally most of us thought of Mr Cook simply and solely as an agitator, and those at any rate in fairly comfortable jobs may be forgiven a very strong dislike of agitations and those which cause them. However, the manner in which Mr Cook has followed up the Housing Question, the interest and time he has given to all phases of it and the sacrifices he seems prepared to make to get something doing and the grasp he had got of the whole subject shows something more than agitator.

Hopefully the impression of A. J. Cook to emerge from this study is that he was indeed 'something more than an agitator'. Nevertheless, his brand of revolutionary fervour was not normally associated with the responsibilities of office. Cook became a major figure within the hierarchy of the largest district of the SWMF, with some 40,000 members. At the age of thirty-seven he joined Noah Ablett and S. O. Davies (in 1920 a young miners' agent in Dowlais) as a very select band of agents whose qualities seemed incongruous with the attributes traditionally associated with leadership in the South Wales coalfield. As Peter Stead has pointed out, SWMF leaders tended to be secretaries rather than generals, with administrative and financial skills harnessed to a moderate industrial philosophy. These characteristics are not normally associated with zealots like Arthur Cook. *The Miners' Next Step* had criticised the nature and role of miners' agents, accusing them of sacrificing the interests of their members for their personal quest for respectability and prestige. In 1920 Cook became a white-collar worker, with a briefcase, an office and a desk. His salary was nearly double the average earnings of a miner. His work entailed routine administration as well as negotiations with coalowners and managers concerning a variety of disputes. Under the strains of power, responsibility and work-load, many miners' agents compromised earlier convictions and became bastions of conservatism. But Arthur Cook was an example of the new breed of miners' leader which had emerged in response to changed economic and political conditions. He was not to be shackled or corrupted by power; rather than joining the ranks of the moderates he used his enhanced power to attack and embarrass them. His syndicalist ambitions probably made him a blunt and blatant negotiator, lacking the subtlety of an old hand, but his leadership seemed suited to the heady days of 1920 in the Rhondda.

By virtue of his election Cook gained a seat on the SWMF Executive Council and official access to MFGB conferences. From this position he was able to play a significant role in the dramatic events of 1920 and 1921. They began with an URC-led campaign for large wage increases and shorter hours in line with *The Miners' Next Step's* programme of absorbing the coal industry's profits as a preliminary to workers' control of the mines. At the same time, of course, such an adventurous policy promised welcome improvements in the miners' living standards, which rising prices threatened to erode. The URC/SWSS group was very active in the early months of 1920; the Home Office Directorate of Intelligence noted with alarm that the extremists of the URC had been planning a strike and negotiating with shops and co-operative societies about food supplies to strikers. The strike was to be the precursor to revolution, and soldiers were 'to be invited not to shoot'. A press report of one of his meetings reveals Cook's platform behaviour and his message at this time: 'He kept the audience rocked with laughter at times, and as he paced the platform with uplifted arms he warned his hearers of the coming relolution.'

March 1920 saw the TUC's rejection of a call for a general strike in support of mines nationalisation. The URC group, never supportive of nationalisation *per se,* now stepped up demands for a £2 a week wage increase designed to absorb the industry's profits. Arthur Cook made his first speech at a MFGB conference on 12 March, and struck a typically militant note with an attack on the Executive Committee's recommendation of a 3*s* per day claim:

> we have based our demand on a certain surplus, we are told here we must be businessmen, and we are talking about the regulation of wages and the guaranteeing of profits in the Miners' Federation of Great Britain, instead of representing trade unionists, instead of guaranteeing to those we represent a living. . . we want £2 a week to meet the increased cost of living, and to use the general power of the organisation to raise the status of the men.[12]

Such syndicalist demands did not appeal to the MFGB conference delegates, who backed the Executive's 3*s* a day claim. The government, however, would not meet this, offering a twenty-per-cent increase. Following pressure from the militants, with Cook and S. O. Davies to the fore, the MFGB Executive decided to press ahead with their demand. Arthur Cook was delighted that 'we are going to use the power of this organisation to obtain it', even though he had previously criticised the amount claimed. The militants were confident that strike action would be taken, but when the government offered a compromise twenty-per-cent increase with a guaranteed 2*s* a day, the membership voted narrowly in favour of acceptance.

Cook and the militants soon had another opportunity to press for aggressive action, however. The government decided to raise the price of coal; furthermore in the three months up to June 1920 the cost of living had risen by twenty per cent. The MFGB Executive pressed for the cancellation of the coal price increases and a 2*s* a day wage increase. Cook and the URC favoured a straight 4*s* a day wage claim. It had become apparent, however, that inflation was outstripping the coal industry's ability to finance commensurate wage increases. At a MFGB conference in July it was revealed that only the Northumberland, Durham, South Wales and Yorkshire coalfields (where much of the coal was exported) were making a profit. The government, worried that only a small drop in export prices would extinguish that profit, rejected the MFGB's demands and raised the possibility of wage increases dependent on increased output. In September the miners voted heavily in favour of strike action to achieve their 2*s* a day claim.

The growing tension within the South Wales coalfield was supplemented from August onwards by national events outside the mining industry. The National Council of Action was formed following demonstrations against the possibility of British action against the revolutionary government in Russia. The South Wales Marxists viewed the Council of Action as a potentially revolutionary organisation: Noah Ablett told his large audience in Swansea that he was confident the Council of Action would eventually become the real government. The National Council of Action, of course, was no revolutionary cabal, manned as it was by labour leaders who were firm adherents to the sanctity of constitutional methods; evidence also shows that most of the local Councils of Action created throughout Britain shared the limited aspirations of the central body. There were some local Councils, however, who regarded themselves as embryonic soviets. Unsurprisingly, South Wales provided some clear instances of such revolutionary ambition. The Home Office Directorate of Intelligence kept a

close watch on developments in the coalfield, and they recorded
that

> An interesting example of local organisation is provided by Merthyr
> Borough Council of Action, which has been formed for 'the organi-
> sation of industrial workers to function in time of crisis'. The prime
> mover is Noah Ablett (with S. O Davies) . . . The Rhondda 'Council
> of Action' is formed on similar lines, and co-operation between the
> two bodies has been established. A. J. Cook is prime mover in the
> Rhondda Council, and in conjunction with Davies and Ablett, will
> use the new movement as a preliminary to the establishment of the
> Soviet system of government.[13]

Following the waning of the threat of military intervention against
the Bolsheviks many left-wing dominated, Marxist-influenced
local Councils of Action called for an extension of the National
Council's compass to force the withdrawal of troops from Ireland.
Many South Wales Councils made this demand; the Rhondda
Council of Action did so in December. The national Council
refused to act on such demands, however, and in the early months
of 1921 the whole movement withered away. Long before then,
however, events in the mining industry had recaptured the
limelight and demanded Arthur Cook's full attention.

In the summer of 1920 Cook was also involved in the parochial
and convoluted manoeuverings between the various strands of
the British revolutionary movement. The division within the
SWSS came to a head when the society became involved in the
negotiations which led to the formation of the Communist Party
of Great Britain (CPGB). Towards the end of 1918 negotiations
had begun between the British Socialist party (BSP), the Socialist
Labour Party (SLP) and the ILP on the subject of forming a
united communist party. The ILP soon withdrew from the negotiations and was replaced by Sylvia Pankhurst's Workers' Socialist
Federation (WSF) and the nascent SWSS. Immediate difficulties

arose concerning the questions of affiliation to the Labour Party and parliamentary activity. The SWSS joined the WSF and SLP in opposing linkage with Labour, while the WSF opposed *any* parliamentary activity. These tactical differences were reflected within the ranks of the SWSS. Many ILP members of the Society opposed joining a communist party; BSP members wanted a communist party affiliated to Labour; SLP members wanted an independent party undertaking electoral activity; compromisers supported Lenin's advice – that while he was opposed to affiliation with Labour this should not be allowed to stand in the way of forming a united party; and others – those with syndicalist beliefs like Arthur Cook – adopted the WSF position. The SWSS broke up under the strain of such internal divisions, and while most of the SWSS members merged with the groups that formed the CPGB in August, a strict syndicalist anti-political section, in which Arthur Cook and George Dolling were prominent, formed the Communist Party of South Wales and the West of England (CPSWWE). The CPSWWE affiliated to the anti-political Communist Party (British Section of the Third International) formed by Sylvia Pankhurst. The tenets of the CPSWWE, as was explained in a circular to left-wing groups in the region, were the overthrow of capitalism and the establishment of communism, the dictatorship of the proletariat, the forming of Soviets, affiliation to the Third International, and refusal to engage in parliamentary action. When the CPBSTI merged with the CPGB in January 1921, however, Cook and the CPSWWE joined also. It is certain that Cook remained opposed to the CPGB's views on parliamentary action and its attempts to gain affiliation to the Labour Party. In mid-July 1920 Cook wrote in Pankhurst's journal *Worker's Dreadnought* and described himself as 'a communist'. Cook's communism was of an idiosyncratic form, however. It was founded on his deep-rooted desire for an egalitartian society, his acceptance of Marxist economic theory, and admiration of

Lenin's achievements. On this basis Cook was able to call himself a communist all his life. But in other respects Cook was not a communist at all; he rejected the need for a political party: to him the CPSWWE and CPBSTI were no more than clearing-houses for the industrial movement. He supported the formation of local soviets, but these were to be based on the trades councils and fulfil the syndicalist function of co-ordinating the seizure of industry. As Dr Woodhouse pointed out in his study of South Wales rank and file movements the root motive for the development of anti-political communist parties was the desire to 'find a form of organisation that would express the purely industrial character of the URC and which would not be subject to centralised political control'. Most socialist and communist thinkers stress the need for a centralised political party, and indeed Lenin was most adamant on this point. Cook's ideas may be regarded as unsophisticated, short-sighted and naïve, therefore. But the character of Cook's environment, the apparent omnipotence of trade unions – particularly the giant MFGB – inspired such syndicalist confidence; there simply wasn't any *need,* Cook would have argued, for political action – the workers had their unions, and together they could achieve revolutionary changes. The defeats of 1921 and 1926 were imminent, yet in 1920 they were unthinkable to Cook and his generation.

In September 1920 the MFGB sought a negotiated settlement before their strike was due to start. The national leadership reduced their demands but found the government insistent on a pay deal linked to increased output. In the Rhondda Arthur Cook campaigned against any dilution of the MFGB's demands. At a MFGB Special Conference on 23 September he made an impassioned appeal for resoluteness, describing himself as 'a young man who has placed his whole faith in this organisation'. Following further unsuccessful negotiations the MFGB conference five days later heard eloquent speeches from Welsh delegates – Cook, Ablett, Davies and Barker – in favour of strike action. The conference decided to hold another ballot on the government's offer of 1s or 2s per shift dependent on output. Back in the Rhondda Cook and the militants urged members to reject the offer. The result was over-whelming: 635,098 to 181,428 against the terms nationally, and a crushing 158,432 to 22,006 rejection in South Wales. At a MFGB Special Conference in October Arthur Cook rose to second the Executive's recommendation of immediate strike action.

During the 'Datum Line' strike Cook and the URC were very busy. There is evidence to suggest the URC was campaigning seriously for the seizure of collieries. At Tonyrefail Cook persuaded a conference of local miners' lodges to demand the take-over of the pits by the Triple Industrial Alliance. The syndicalists achieved nothing more than scanty, localised support, however, and negotiations at national level soon dominated the miners' thoughts. The government quickly improved their offer to 2s a shift, but insisted that further increases would have to be paid for by greater output. It also announced plans for district committees on which workmen and managers were to co-operate in an effort to promote higher production. To the fury of the militants, the MFGB Executive decided to ballot the men on this offer. Cook worked furiously to generate opposition to the government terms: he promised he would work to destroy the proposed output committees, and showed his disgust with the national leadership by raising once again the question of union reorganisation. The miners voted against the government offer by a very narrow majority, but the MFGB Executive invoked the Federation's two thirds majority rule and recommended termination of the strike and acceptance of the offer. The foisting of the government's terms onto the majority incensed Cook and other militants, but the MFGB conference accepted the Executive's

45

recommendation.

This shabby conclusion of the strike was resented strongly in South Wales. Rank and file confidence in William Brace and Vernon Hartshorn, the two SWMF representatives on the MFGB Executive, was shaken. In November Home Office sources reported that 'revolutionaries like A. J. Cook are consolidating their position', and prophesied resignations by 'the more responsible officials'. Cook in fact emerged as the clear leader of the militants when he spearheaded a verbal onslaught on the MFGB leadership, whom he dubbed 'the lieutenants of the capitalist class', with Hartshorn being singled out for particular condemnation. It appears that a newspaper was launched as an instrument of this campaign: *The Workers' Bomb* was first issued in November 1920, taking its title from the nickname of the pre-war *Rhondda Socialist*. An article by Cook entitled 'The Great Awakening! The Coal Crisis and its Lessons' dominated the front page. The article was a lucid denunciation of the MFGB Executive's handling of the coal dispute, and was shot through with an argument for reorganisation of trade unions on democratic lines as suggested by the URC almost a decade earlier. He expressed the need for the reform of the MFGB 'from the bottom up', and attacked the whole structure of working-class representation: 'The MFGB, Triple Alliance and TUC are fast becoming manufacturing centres for resolutions – glorified state institutions earning the praise of the capitalist class. We are led at the heels of the politicians, the atmosphere of the House of Commons is pervading the trade union executives. The very machine we have built up for our salvation is being used to crush us.' The article's resemblance to passages in *The Miners' Next Step* is striking, and shows Cook's conviction that the rank and file should control their own destiny. In the bitter aftermath of the 'Datum Line' debacle it was a persuasive argument. The official leadership were both alarmed and angry. Hartshorn replied by calling Cook 'the biggest fool in the coalfield' and offering his resignation; he was joined in this display of pique by William Brace. The resignations were accepted by the SWMF Executive. In contrast, the Rhondda No. 1 District meeting passed an unanimous vote of confidence in Arthur Cook. Yet again the familiar undercurrent of dissatisfaction with the union structure came to the fore as Cook and Ablett led an URC campaign for reform of the SWMF by addressing meetings throughout the Rhondda. Writing in *The Workers' Bomb* Cook echoed *The Miners' Next Step* once more with a call for centralisation of the SWMF with rank and file control: 'We cannot hope to control the mining industry before we control our own organisation. The rank and file must have the first and last word.'

Cook's pleas for union reform proved to be the last shots in the syndicalist offensive. Towards the end of 1920 the miners turned the Datum Line corner and then hit a brick wall of economic disaster. In December the price of coal on export markets fell by fifty per cent. Collieries throughout Britain had their profit margins swept away. The government, anxious not to be lumbered with a golden goose that had turned into a liability, hinted that control of the coal industry would be handed back to the owners during 1921. The advances in wages achieved by the miners since 1914 were threatened. For militants like Arthur Cook, the theory that 'we can only get what we are strong enough to win and retain' implied painful consequences when the miners' bargaining power was weakened by the arrival of mass unemployment. Nineteen-twenty saw the zenith and dissipation of the post-war hopes of revolution. Cook, as a professional trade union leader, was forced to abandon his stance as an aggressive Welsh Lenin; instead he was obliged to lead a bewildered army in a desperate rearguard action against attack on their living standards. The year 1920 had been full of changes and dramatic events for Arthur Cook; 1921 was to be no less eventful, but far more painful.

3   *The road to Russell Square*

During the first three months of 1921 each ton of coal raised in Great Britain made a loss of 7s. The rapid fall in export prices was reflected in the fact that the loss per ton in South Wales was 19s 9d. Unemployment swept through the valleys. By mid-January half the pits in South Wales were on short-time, and by March half the miners in the Rhondda were out of work. At the end of January the Cabinet decided to decontrol the coal industry in two months' time. The MFGB was informed officially one month later, just five weeks before the coalowners regained control of the industry.

This catastrophic start to the new year coincided with a further step forward in the career of Arthur Cook. George Barker was elected MP for Abertillery and consequently resigned his position as SWMF representative on the MFGB Executive. Cook was chosen to replace Barker, and he attended his first Executive meeting on 29 January. Recently a harsh critic of the Executive's actions, Cook found himself a member of that powerful body, at the very centre of the Federation's leadership. Together with Ablett, Cook brought syndicalism to the highest level of the union; but this happened at a time when visions of workers' control had been swept away and replaced by the realities of mass unemployment and the inevitable attacks on miners' wages and conditions.

On 22 February a MFGB conference met to discuss the problem of unemloyment. James Winstone moved a South Wales resolution calling for measure 'to get the whole Labour Movement to take drastic action within fourteen days' to enforce government remedies. Arthur Cook rose to second the resolution; his speech revealed his continuing belief in syndicalist tactics, but with half the Rhondda unemployed his words have in retrospect an unrealistic ring:

> I am coming to the conclusion, after the last two months, that all virtue has gone out of this Federation. It seems to me, looking back and seeing the growth of trade unions, that with that growth and power there seems to be a lack of fighting spirit. . . I have been trying to analyse this matter and have come to the conclusion that we cannot solve this problem (of unemployment) under the present system. . . our policy for the Labour Party Conference tomorrow should be to urge the whole Labour movement to take action.
>
> I am told by many older men that we must try again constitutional methods, that is Parliament. . . That is why we are getting no further. If we cannot move Parliament to do something, we ought to be able to do it ourselves. We have been talking about control of the industry. . . We have first of all to destroy the system, if we have come to the conclusion there is no solution under the present system. . . We may not solve the problem by a general strike, we may have intensified or increased it, but we shall have brought it to a head, then will come the situation whether we as organised Labour have to tell the democracy whether we can take over the industries.[1]

His response was typical of Marxists who viewed the dramatic onset of mass unemployment as evidence of the impending collapse of capitalism. But the nature of the 1921 crisis was misinterpreted, and the durability of capitalism underestimated. The arrival of deep economic depression did not produce a revolutionary situation. Cook's talk of a general strike and the potential for workers' control was, in the circumstances, impractical wishful thinking. The day after Cook's speech the miners were informed of the government's decontrol date. All talk of improvement, and cetainly all hopes of revolution or the taking over of collieries, disappeared. The miners realised that any fight now would be for the status quo. In South Wales the coalowners made it clear that decontrol would be accompanied by large wage reductions, and Cook was active in stiffening resistence amongst the Rhondda miners. On Sunday 6 March he addressed meetings at Cymmer, Porth and Ynyshir during which he appealed for united trade union action to fight any attempted reductions. He informed his audiences that unless they organised for a fight the miners would have to accept a fifty per cent wage cut at the end of March.

At a national level, the Mining Association intimated that the national profits and wages agreement which operated under government control would have to be abandoned. The coalowners felt such national machinery 'strengthened the hands of the nationalisers' and would be 'fatal to efficiency and enterprise' as it involved the subsidisation of loss-making areas by the profitable. The MFGB, however, cherished the national structure – it satisfied their ideological commitment to the principle of 'equal pay for equal work' irrespective of geological and productive differentials. Both owners and union also recognised that national agreements enhanced the bargaining power of the MFGB – when a national wages agreement expired, the whole weight of the Federation could be brought to bear on the employers. In place of national agreements the Mining Association wished to revert to the system whereby each area would negotiate wage level commensurate with that district's ability to pay. The consequences of this method for miners in South Wales, where coal was being mined at a loss of £1 per ton, were clearly disastrous.

On 18 March a MFGB Special Conference debated the bleak future. Many Executive members, including the new President Herbert Smith and the General Secretary Frank Hodges, favoured a temporary return to district agreements so that area associations would be free to negotiate the best terms possible. Arthur Cook, however, all too aware of the impact of such a move on the men he represented, declared that 'we have not given up the idea of a National Board'. On 21 March a MFGB conference decided to seek the retention of the national wage machinery; according to Herbert Smith this was 'a declaration of war'.

Home Office intelligence reports reveal that Cook ('this man is the leader of the extremists on the South Wales Executive') and the URC were actively promoting rank and file support for the national agreement. They were unlikely to meet much opposition once the coalowners' proposals were known. As Cook had predicted, wage reductions of nearly fifty per cent were demanded in South Wales. The MFGB Executive, though prepared to tolerate limited wage cuts in line with the fall in the cost of living, were emphatic in their opposition to the massive reductions proposed in many coalfields. On the eve of decontrol the Executive decided to allow the owners' lock-out notices to expire 'regardless of occupation'. For the Executive, even with Cook and Ablett present, this was a very militant decision: it meant that safety workers – those responsible for the prevention of flooding and the feeding of pit ponies – were to be withdrawn. Over one million men were locked out. Before disbanding to the districts the MFGB Executive resolved to ask the Triple Alliance to take sympathetic strike action; back in the Rhondda, Cook urged local railwaymem and transport workers to join the fight: 'Labour throughout the country must realize this was the acid test by which their future would be assured or their downfall effected.' He appeared confident that a united, determined, trade union movement could defeat the coalowners and government.

Such faith appeared justified when the miners' allies in the Triple Alliance decided to strike on 12 April. But the leaders of the MFGB's partners were anxious to extricate their unions from this action. They persuaded the MFGB Executive to order back the safetymen as an entrée to further negotiations. When the talks proved fruitless the railwaymen and transport leaders reluctantly decided not to abandon the miners, and set another date for strike action. With other unions also expressing support for the MFGB, a strike of massive proportions seemed imminent. The four South Wales members of the Federation Executive issued a message to their men, and the text bore the imprint of the two syndicalists, Cook and Ablett:

> Unable to meet your arguments, or to counter the irresistible moral force of your claim for a living wage, the Government have called up soldiers, sailors and airmen, and are actively recruiting a British White Guard. They little know you who think that you can be overawed by displays of armed force. If the spirit of militarism has migrated from the Wilhelmstrasse to Whitehall, the British nation still retains its belief in the fundamental futility of violence. . .
>
> Trust simply and solely in your economic power, in the wholehearted support of your comrades of the Triple Alliance and of other Trade Unions, and in the great and growing body of public opinion outside the ranks of organised labour, which is convinced that the scale of wages which the mineowners and the Government seeks to thrust upon you is shameful and intolerable. We were locked out together, we will remain out together, we will return together.[2]

But the trust in the Triple Alliance was misplaced. At a meeting with MPs on 14 April Frank Hodges was reported to have said that the MFGB would be prepared to adandon temporarily the national agreement. The miners' allies seized upon the alleged remarks as a pretext for calling off their sympathetic strike. This was on 'Black Friday', 15 April.

With the miners now alone, the MFGB Executive members, who had been in London for over a fortnight, returned to their districts to help organise the struggle. Cook addressed meetings throughout the Rhondda in which he reported events over the previous two weeks. Further negotiations in London later that month reached deadlock, and the dispute became a war of attrition. According to Robin Page Arnot, the miners' struggle was 'conducted under such conditions of governmental repression as had scarcely been known since well-nigh a century';[3] many arrests were made in the mining communities, and the authorities were not reticent in dealing with Federation leaders. Arthur Cook soon attracted special attention from his old adversaries, Capt. Lionel Lindsay and his deputy John Williams. In the second week of May the windows of Cook's house in Porth were smashed during the night, frightening his twelve-year-old son. Cook took the boy to stay with relatives in Bristol, and while he was away his house was raided by the police. The *Rhondda Leader* reported that:

> Quite a sensation was caused in the Rhondda Valley on Saturday (14 May) when it became known that raids had been made upon the homes of prominent local federationists. About 2.15 pm, Deputy Chief Constable John Williams, acting upon the instructions of Captain Lionel Lindsay, visited the house of A. J. Cook at Nyth Bran, Porth, in company with several other officers, and took away a large quantity of correspondence.

At the end of May Cook was charged at Pontypridd with inciting to intimidate a safety worker during a speech at Ynyshir, inciting to disturb the peace, and unlawful assembly. As in 1918, Cook's companion in the dock was George Dolling. The prosecution claimed that both defendants addressed a crowd of 3,000 at Ynyshir, and that Cook had described safetymen as blacklegs and stated they must be treated as such. Cook and Dolling were committed for trial, but released on £30 bail.

By the beginning of June, after nearly ten weeks of the lock-out there was widespread suffering in the coalfields. Soup kitchens were established in most mining towns and villages. Under these circumstances the MFGB decided to ballot its members on whether they should fight on. In the Rhondda Cook told meetings that the government offer of a £10 million subsidy was 'a substantial advance, though far from satisfactory'. The SWMF leadership, including Cook and Ablett, had concluded reluctantly that better terms could not be won. But the bravery and spirit of the mining communities was revealed when the ballot vote produced overwhelming rejection of the government offer. The fight went on.

Cook, meanwhile, had made another appearance in Pontypridd Police Court to face trial on the charge of inciting to disturb the peace; the other charges were postponed to a future trial. At the hearing 'remarkable illustrations of the activity of the revolutionary forces in this country' were quoted when the prosecution read documents taken from Cook's home by the police. Correspondence revealed that Cook was a very active member of the CPGB. The case against Cook was dismissed, however: the magistrate explained that there were violent expressions in some of Cook's speeches but there had been a recent lull which suggested that he had 'run through a period of wild oats as a labour leader' and had 'found salvation in something saner'. It is hard to avoid the conclusion that Cook's recommendation of the government's offer kept him out of prison in June. But Cook's 'salvation' was an illusion. On 18 June the MFGB Executive debated policy in the light of the ballot: Noah Ablett proposed the withdrawal of safetymen; Cook suggested that another attempt be made to join forces with other unions – the Executive accepted both tactics. Cook regarded it as his duty to implement the 'fight on' message of the membership even though he had recommended acceptance of the terms offered. All traces of defeatism disappeared from his public statements:

> The fight is now going to be of a totally different character. The whole body of miners is going to conduct a struggle for the sociali-

sation or nationalisation of the mines. It is going to be and must be, a fight directly against the Government. The feeling of the miners of the country is such that, even if it means smashing the present system, they are not prepared to go any further into these impossible terms. The men are still imbued with the idea of a national pool, because they believe in nationalisation. It seems quite clear now that it will be impossible to get peace with the mining industry under private ownership.[4]

It is revealing to note Cook's apparently sudden support for nationalisation, and apart from the relevance of Cook's remarks to the lock-out, his statement signalled a shift in his industrial philosophy. The syndicalist tactic of 'encroaching control' had been discredited by the consequences of economic depression in 1921. Henceforth Cook's belief in workers' control was increasingly regarded as dependent on the attainment of the MFGB's official target of nationalisation. But talk of nationalisation at a time when hunger gnawed at the mining communities was mere bravado. Characteristically, Cook reacted to the prospect of defeat by attempting to boost the morale of the miners, often by painting an over-optimistic picture for them. His conference speeches were often far colder, reasoned appraisals of the miners' strategic position. Such realism was required when it became obvious that, with support from other unions unforthcoming, the miners were being starved into submission. Towards the end of June the MFGB Executive re-opened negotiations and achieved a slightly improved offer. The Executive accepted the proposals on the men's behalf without a ballot, and called off the strike. The miners returned to work defeated after three months' struggle. For Cook and other militants, confidence in united trade union action had been destroyed by the betrayal perpetrated by leaders like J. H. Thomas. The lesson, if it was not known before, was clear – the MFGB could not win alone. And yet, 'Black Friday' had shown that sympathetic action by other unions was

not automatically forthcoming. For Cook and many other militants, faith in an industrial alliance was shaken but not broken –
they concluded that the structure of any future alliance must be
strengthened. But Cook believed in organised rertreat before a
stronger opponent; as he said in another context, 'we must have
our Mons'. So Cook advised a return to work in July; he showed
an ability to recognise weakness as well as strength. This was a
quality of Cook's leadership which has not been appreciated by
historians.

Cook's pragmatic leadership during the 1921 dispute was not
appreciated in all quarters – he was subjected to unprecedented
criticism from left-wing elements in the Rhondda. He had
opposed the CPGB's policy of 'fight to the finish'; he even
reproached his members who had failed to realise the hopelessness
of further struggle. Two Rhondda lodges called for Cook's resignation as agent. Later in July the Home Office Intelligence
Department accomplished a remarkable feat of infiltration when
it reported that

> A. J. Cook informed the Porth Branch (of the CPGB) on July 17th
> that he was definitely resigning his membership of the Communist
> Party 'because the Party wanted weeding, at present there were
> too many undesirables, as it were, within its ranks'. Cook added
> that although he would no longer be a member of the Party he was
> always there actively to support and assist it and, if necessary, speak
> for it.[5]

Cook's leadership had been condemned within the CPGB's
national executive, and it seems there was a degree of CP-inpired
criticism within some SWMF lodges, but demands for his resignation came to nothing.

Before Cook had officially announced his resignation from the
CPGB he appeared again in court, facing trial on the charges left
outstanding from June. Cook denied the statements attributed

to him by the police in evidence, and claimed he had opposed the withdrawal of safety workers. Nevertheless he was found guilty and sentenced to two months' hard labour for inciting to intimidate a safetyman and unlawful assembly. Such was the toll of vengeance exacted by the authorities in the immediate aftermath of the miners' defeat. George Dolling, who had made a habit of appearing in the same dock as Arthur Cook, was sentenced to four months' hard labour (perhaps he advised the men to fight on), while at Maerdy forty miners (including most of the lodge officials) were arrested. Arthur Horner, one of those found guilty and sentenced to prison, recalled his experience vividly:

> We were housed in Swansea for the night, and Arthur Cook, who had been sentenced earlier in the Assizes, was with us. The next day they put us in chains. They handcuffed each man and chained six of us together. We were taken from Swansea prison to Cardiff prison. It was a holiday weekend and Cardiff station was packed with people going off for the day. There we were in the middle of the holiday crowd im chains. . .
>
> In Cardiff prison, I was put on the job of scrubbing the steps and the lower landing. The others, including Arthur Cook, were put to pick oakum. They used to have to pick a pound a day, and one day Arthur Cook arrived with both hands holding a mass of fluffy oakum as it looked like after it had been picked. The Warder took it from, screwed it up into a tiny ball, and said, 'A bloody bird could do more than that.'[6]

The situation may have contained some humour, but Cook found the experience humiliating and it left an emotional mark on him. When he was released on 1 September he was far from jovial, and in a 'message to the workers' published in the *Rhondda Leader* he vented his pent-up anger:

> I have had a unique though trying experience this year, my adventures taking me to the Downing Street parlour, Police and Assize Courts, and finally to the prison cell as a guest of His Majesty. Several lodge officials with myself have been separated from their loved ones, compelled to wear the broad arrow, and treated precisely the same as the lowest of low criminals. All this, doubtlessly, is intended to forcibly demonstrate the Coalition's contention that there us no class war. Despite faith and confidence in me on the part of the workers, it seems I am to be continually haunted and oppressed by the police at all my meetings, and my wife and children terrorised. All because I stand for the emancipation of the working class.

Cook's resignation from the CPGB was announced officially towards the end of September. He complained of the party's 'interference' in the lock-out, and described the Communists as 'a hindrance to the whole of the British Trade Union Movement'. He predicted that 'we shall eventually have to fight the Communist Party'. It is interesting to speculate whether Cook's resignation was due entirely to the CP's activities during the lock-out. It is feasible that the reason for his original reluctance to join the CPGB was also a factor. Cook was different from Horner and other members of the URC/SWSS faction who joined the CPGB at the end of 1920. Horner, for example, found his ideological home in the Party – he was on its Central Committee in 1923 and remained a lifelong member. For Cook, however, as pointed out in the previous chapter, the CPGB was relevant for its contribution to the industrial struggle, not as a political party *per se*. The concept of having union leadership subject to central political control was abhorrent to Cook. Despite his close ties with the CP throughout the next seven years, Cook never rejoined it.

For the remainder of 1921 and most of 1922 Cook's leadership lacked its usual militancy. Real wages were significantly below the 1914 level, while the large reduction of labour costs did not prevent widespread colliery closures. In South Wales wages fell by over fifty per cent. Unemployment, low wages and demoralisation decimated the SWMF: membership fell from 197,000 at the end of 1920 to 87,000 at the end of 1922. The number of SWMF representatives on the MFGB Executive fell as a result, and Arthur Cook lost his seat. The man who had risen to prominence during the post-war flaring of militancy, and whose oratorical powers had fired up the Rhondda, now spoke to half-empty halls. At Ton Pentre in October 1921 he asked a small gathering, 'don't you think it is time to wake up? There won't be much trouble over income tax for the future, because the miners will not get enough to warrant the payment'. Under such miserable circumstances Cook's support for aggressive policies evaporated. In common with Ablett and Davies he accepted there was no immediate prospect of overturning the July 1921 wages agreement. Co-operation with employers had been anathema to Arthur Cook before the lock-out, but in its aftermath he was willing to swallow his natural distaste for conciliation in order to protect jobs. In fact he was prepared, for the first time in his life, to urge miners to boost output and accept the double shift system previously strongly resisted in South Wales. He met pit managers who threatened closure, and was prepared to promise them improved productivity if they kept operating. It was a startling reversal of his pre-lock-out leadership; and it was born out of desperation and the desire to ease the suffering amongst miners and their families. However, whatever the merits of the motives behind Cook's transformed policy, it lost him some friends. The Maerdy lodge contained men who had shared a prison sentence with Cook, including his closest friend Arthur Horner who was the lodge's vice-chairman. But the Maerdy committee was disgusted by Cook's moderation and called for his resignation. Cook went up to meet the lodge committee and apologised for remarks he made in the press which attempted to minimise the seriousness of disputes at Maerdy. But this episode did not make Cook abandon his co-operative policy. As late as June 1922 he was informing meetings that there was no hope of wage increases or full-time working, and he pleaded with miners not to rush into precipitate action: 'It was essential that the South Wales miners, in whatever policy they pursued, should act in conjunction with the MFGB and, if possible, with the whole trade union movement.'

The second half of 1922 saw an important shift in attitude amongst SWMF and MFGB officials. The policy of co-operation with the employers had been seen to fail; the coalowners had seized upon their strong position to drive down colliery price lists, encourage non-unionism and implement a ruthless attitude towards unemployment. Miners' leaders realised there was little to be gained from conciliation; instead most union officials, even moderates, sought to repair and rebuild the Federation's strength as a prerequisite of and prelude to a more aggressive policy. At the same time the revolutionary elements within the South Wales coalfield revived, and focused on propaganda for MFGB affiliation to the Communist Red International of Labour Unions (RILU) instead of the non-revolutionary Amsterdam International Federation of Trade Unions. While CPGB members provided the impetus at lodge level, fellow-travellers like Cook, Ablett and Davies played a prominent part in the movement. At the MFGB Annual Conference in July 1922 Cook made a long speech in favour of affiliation to the RILU which showed that his prime motive was industrial: he wanted to see an effective international trade union organisation which could be of assistance to the MFGB during a dispute. Certainly this was not the point at which Cook's *rapprochement* with the CPGB was completed – in fact he claimed that the RILU was not connected with the Communist Party. Perhaps this denial of CP involvement was an attempt to overcome the anti-communist feelings of many of the MFGB conference delegates; if so, he failed – only the South Wales contingent voted in favour.

The pro-RILU movement in South Wales did not achieve its prime purpose. But it dragged the left wing on the coalfield out of its post-lock-out mire. The failure of the co-operative approach and the long-term, international character of the depression in the coal trade convinced many thinking miners that union strength must be restored. For Arthur Cook the months of demoralisation and conciliation gave way to a more positive spirit. He firmly believed that negotiations were always decided by the relative strengths of the two sides; the re-establishment of the MFGB's capacity to fight and win was the aim now. Meanwhile, wounds had to be licked and those who thirsted for revenge had to be patient. At a MFGB conference in December 1922 called to consider whether the Federation should terminate the 1921 agreement Cook made his strategy clear:

> I am convinced that if we give notice to end the agreement with the object of changing it, to negotiate with the employers, that is asking for conflict. The employers, as you have already heard, whether or not they are serious in the matter I don't know, have put forward a request for a reduction of the minimum (wage). The question we have to face is, are we in a position industrially as a Miners' Federation to enter that conflict? If when we were strong we failed to get the pool and unification, can we get it now? . . . I am inclined to believe it is possible that we could put up a fight if we could only reconsider our positions as miners hand in hand with the trade unions of this country on the recommendation of the (TUC) General Council. Personally, I am very much afraid that the miners alone cannot enter a conflict for the living wage. . . I am a little bit cautious now. Conditions determine largely a man's actions, and let me say to my friends in Scotland or Wales that we have to live along with the times.[7]

Such level-headed leadership does not match the traditional picture of Cook as a mountain torrent of revolutionary oratory. But it did not signal the end of Cook's career as a militant: in fact the next eighteen months saw Cook re-emerge as a leading advocate of a fighting policy, and events were to catapult him to national notoriety.

During the winter of 1922-3 an unexpected upturn occurred in the fortunes of the coal industry. A miners' strike in the USA and the French occupation of the Ruhr created an artificially high demand for British coal. Unemployment amongst miners faded as quickly as it had arrived, but under the 1921 agreement wages did not recover sufficiently to erase the hardship of miners' families. Under such conditions the MFGB recaptured some of its ambition. In South Wales the Federation launched a campaign against non-unionism, and in April the Rhondda District struck work on the issue. Arthur Cook's leadership reflected the determination of the union to reverse the tide that had been running against it. He warned the men that the employers were 'out to smash to Federation', and urged non-unionists to go 'back to the union'. When the Rhondda strike ended membership had climbed from 18,000 to 40,000 in the two valleys. Cook also revived the pressure for SWMF affiliation to the RILU, but this movement soon gave way to a far larger national organisation which dominated left-wing industrial politics in the coalfields until the General Strike. The Miners' Minority Movement (MMM) was CPGB-inspired but catered also for the non-CP left and thus provided a natural ideological home for Arthur Cook. It suited his industrial philosophy while allowing him an informal alliance with the Communist Party. His association with the MMM was to be mutually beneficial – Minority Movement support played an important part in Cook's election as MFGB General Secretary in 1924, and from that position Cook became an important mouthpiece for the movement.

On 27 October 1923 the inaugural conference of the South Wales Miners' minority Movement took place. The Chief Constable of Cardiff informed the Special Branch that Cook was one of the convenors of the conference, and that he claimed the Minority Movement has a legitimate role as 'the advance guard' in the SWMF, and that half the Executive Committee was connected with it. His friend Arthur Horner chaired the conference, but it was Cook who became the Minority Movement's most vocal figure. At first the MMM concentrated on the immediate problems of wages and conditions; writing in the CPGB's *Workers' Weekly,* Cook declared:

> For over two years the miners of this country, especially in South Wales, have suffered beyond description. The agreement that Frank Hodges blessed has brought poverty and misery to the toilers of the mine. *Patience has been exhausted. Our people refuse to starve peacefully. They claim the right to live, South Wales is preparing for the struggle.*

In a private letter to Arthur Horner that the police gained access to, Cook insisted that 'failing the MFGB, South Wales must act' to end the 1921 wages agreement;[8] in December Cook urged the SWMF conference to press for termination of the agreement, and in the same month wrote an article for the RILU's *All Power* in which he urged miners to 'form Minority Movements in every district, attend all your branch meetings, and let us again rally the miners to the great struggle that is in front of us'.

In January 1924 the MFGB balloted the men on the question of termination of the 1921 agreement: 510,000 voted for termination, 144,000 against it; in South Wales the result was an overwhelming 129,000 to 14,000. The prospect of industrial conflict reappeared. It coincided with the formation of the national Miners' Minority Movement in Sheffield which launched its own newspaper, *The Mineworker,* which first appeared at the end of February. The MMM's programme was straightforward – one industrial miners' union (to replace the federated structure); affiliation to the RILU; a wage equivalent to the 1914 level plus 2*s* per shift; a six-hour day. Cook was the most prominent miners' leader within the MMM and the columns of *The Mineworker,* and soon the movement had another aim – the election of Cook as Secretary of the MFGB.

Also in January Ramsay MacDonald formed the first Labour Government. He employed several moderate union leaders in his administration. Vernon Hartshorn was appointed Postmaster-General. Cook replaced Hartshorn as a SWMF representative on the MFGB Executive. But this move was overtaken by the consequences of Frank Hodges's election as MP for Lichfield. The MFGB's constitution demanded that he resign as general secretary. Despite Hodges's attempt to circumvent the rules, the Federation Executive decided to ask districts for nominations for the vacancy. At this point Cook's co-operation with the MMM and CPGB reached a high level. Militants in the coalfields feared, with ample justification, that the MFGB Executive was flouting the recent ballot vote and prevaricating on the question of obtaining an improved wages agreement. Cook's position on the Executive was of great importance to the MMM. He reported the proceedings of Executive meetings in the Communist press in an effort to arm the rank and file against the moderate leaders; his actions were not restricted by notions of collective responsibility – for example, on the front page of the *Workers' Weekly* of 25 January he urged miners to demand a conference:

> a majority of the present MFGB Executive still believe in the principles of the old agreement and are prepared to negotiate with the employers on the old proposals. They are interpreting the ballot vote to suit their own opinions. . . Comrades of the Miners' Federation, I shall be charged with disloyalty to my colleagues by giving the above information, but I have made up my mind that loyalty to the rank and file comes first. I do not want a repetition of 1921.

In February the SWMF Executive invited nominations from lodges for the MFGB Secretaryship, and announced plans for a ballot on the transferable vote system. Cook's standing within the SWMF would certainly have earned him many nominations, but the support of the South Wales MMM was important if he was to have a real chance of winning. Despite Cook's high profile within the MMM two other redoubtable left-wingers – the venerated Noah Ablett and W. H. Mainwaring (who was a member of the CPGB at this time) – had also been nominated. A conference of the South Wales MMM was convened to debate and decide which candidate it would support. Arthur Horner chaired the meeting and recorded in his autobiography that the voting produced a tie between his mentor Ablett and his close friend Arthur Cook. He gave his casting vote to Cook, and explains why:

> Ablett, I said, was a thoughtful, logical Marxist, who did not bother about personal popularity and who would not fail in anything he decided to try. But I went on to say that I thought he would be inclined to try one path and pursue it to the end. Cook, on the other hand, would examine half a dozen paths, and would try the lot. Perhaps four or even five would fail, but the sixth would win. This, I said, was a time for new ideas. We needed an agitator, a man with a sense of adventure, and I believed Cook was the man.[9]

There many have been other factors which swayed Horner: Cook, as a non-CPGB left winger, may have appeared a candidate with wide appeal. Furthermore, Ablett had built up a reputation as a heavy drinker. Cook also became the choice of the national MMM, and throughout February he was a prolific contributor to MMM and the Communist press. Nevertheless it was the CPGB member Mainwaring who was favourite to win the South Wales nomination ballot. Indeed throughout the early counts Mainwaring led, narrowly at first but by 8,000 votes before the final count, when Ablett was eliminated. That final count, however, revealed that the vast majority of Ablett's transfered votes were in Cook's favour, producing a final result of 50,123–49,617 for Cook. Thus it was Arthur Cook's name that went forward to join a list of eight other candidates nominated throughout the MFGB. With the possible exception of Henry Hicken from the small Derbyshire area, Cook was the only MMM supporter in the field; indeed, the other candidates were known to be moderates.

The background to the national election ballot was one of growing dissatisfaction with living conditions. In March a MFGB conference rejected the coalowners' offer of a twelve-and-a-half per cent increase in the minimum wage, and called on the Labour government to introduce a minimum wage bill to ensure a 'wage commensurate with the cost of living'. In fact the government had already decided to reject a minimum wage bill and proposed to set up a commission of inquiry if negotiations between the MFGB and coalowners broke down. Another MFGB conference on 26 March heard Cook assess the situation and reassert his syndicalist strategy:

> The political door is shut as far as legislation on the Minimum Wage Bill is concerned. . . I am more concerned about the Labour Movement than I am of the Labour Government. . . Then what door is open? The door of an industrial settlement, which means consideration of the terms that we have got from the owners, or the door of an inquiry. . . We are an industrial organisation, and I am going to ask you, as I am, be prepared to face the facts of the situation, and endeavour to extract from the owners the highest possible terms and then consider them as an alternative to a strike. I do not think that a strike should be so feared. . . don't trust this political side, let us trust to our own power and use it to get all we can.

Two days later, however, after the Executive had had unsuccessful talks with the Mining Association, Cook supported the call for a court of inquiry, and although he expressed reservations about such a move, he made it clear he felt the Federation was not yet in a position to strike. The majority of the conference delegates felt the same way, but Cook was again advocating a far less militant line than most of his South Wales colleagues, and his sudden change in tactics must have perplexed them. But it was not the first time and it would not be the last. Obviously Cook could not forget the 1921 lock-out, which revealed the lack of homogeneity within the MFGB, and in particular the varying political attitudes and fighting capabilities of the districts. Cook was aware that some coalfields did not share South Wales's radicalism or its appetite for struggle.

The conference atmosphere at the time of the Secretaryship ballot was one of growing militancy tempered by caution. Amongst the mining communities, however, particularly in the exporting districts, there was rising anger, frustration and bitterness at the deprivation they continued to endure. Cook, as the most renowned militant amongst the candidates, and with the massive South Wales area behind him, led the voting throughout the several counts, although his final margin of victory over Joseph Jones (Yorkshire) was a comparatively narrow 217,000 votes to 202,000. At the age of forty, and only four years since leaving the coal-face, Cook became Secretary of the largest and most powerful union in Britain, responsible for nearly 800,000 members. Cook's response to news of his election was a combination of excitement and awe, mixed with surprise 'that he had attracted so much support from outside South Wales'. *The Mineworker* printed the news in large letters, claiming 'a victory for the MMM'. *The Times,* on the other hand, announced starkly: 'Miners' Secretary – A South Wales Extremist'. The reaction of the leadership of the labour movement can be gauged from the outburst by Fred Bramley, Secretary of the TUC: 'Have you seen who has been elected secretary of the Miners' Federation? Cook, a raving, tearing Communist. Now the miners are in for a bad time.'[10] Perhaps Bramley had just read the *Daily Herald,* to whom

Cook had given his first interview after the ballot result:

> Cook, interviewed, said he took it that the men who voted for him knew his policy – 'that is for industrial unionism, and the carrying out of my work with a regard to Marxian economics and philosophy. I will not rest satisfied until private enterprise in the mining industry is abolished. I know that this can only be accomplished in stages, but I have definitely made it a goal to aim for.'

Cook revealed in this interview his fundamental strategy for the post-1921 reality – the eventual overthrow of capitalism – but the immediate task was to negotiate from a position of strength convinced, as he always had been, that it was 'power that counts'. It is obvious, however, that Cook's reputation as a revolutionary orator blinded most contemporaries and historians to the more calculating and realistic aspects of his leadership. The months ahead were to test Cook's ability to administer the MFGB, present a coherent and well-researched argument, and rouse the morale and fighting strength of the mining communities. As Bramley had forecast, the miners were in for a bad time, but it was to be *despite* the efforts of Arthur Cook. In the words of Robin Page Arnot: 'The choice of him by the miners was eloquent of their sufferings for the past three years. It was a token of spirit undismayed by hardship. It was a choice which meant a renewal of struggle.'[11]

Cook's first months at the MFGB headquarters in Russell Square provided a trying baptism. On the day his election was announced the MFGB Executive also revealed that the miners had voted narrowly against acceptance of the owners' wage proposals. Such a small majority prohibited strike action, and the MFGB asked the government for an inquiry into the wages issue. Cook devoted much of his time to the provision of information for the Federation's case at the inquiry, and performed well while the investigation sat. But he did not believe it would recommend a 'living wage', nor did he expect it to prevent the coalowners from seeking further reductions in labour costs when the temporary recovery ended. In a May Day message in the *Daily Herald* he warned: 'Difficult days are ahead to us – days that will call for solidarity, loyalty and courage. Be firm and loyal to the Federation and the Cause.' The court of inquiry reported on 9 May, and did not recommend specific wage figures, merely that a minimum wage should be the first charge on the industry. When negotiations between the MFGB Executive and the Mining Association resumed, the owners increased their offer from a twelve-and-a-half to a thirteen-and-a-half per cent increase in the minimum wage. The miners were faced with a stark choice· – accept this unsatisfactory offer or take industrial action. The Executive decided to recommend the terms to the men, and Cook agreed. In a speech back in Porth on 18 May he explained that the miners had 'to make the best of a bad job, since the Federation had neither the financial nor trade union support' at that moment. It was, he said, a question of tactics since both the political and industrial doors were closed; it would be wiser to make a short-term compromise and live to fight another day. To make such a speech in his power-base where miners had become accustomed to hardline militancy from their local boy-made-good is further evidence of Cook's ability to adjust his leadership to the circumstances – his advice was not the emotional rambling of a fanatic.

The MMM was confused and dismayed by Cook's tactics, and concluded that he had been swayed by the MFGB Executive against his better judgement. It is ironical that in his first MFGB conference as Secretary Cook led his Executive against the MMM delegates. He was at loggerheads with his former close associate S. O. Davies, and when the vote was taken the large minority who opposed acceptance of the owners' terms included the South Wales delegation. Cook's awareness of the MFGB's vulnerable

69

position had – as in 1921 – strained his relationship with the far left in the union.

But Cook differed from other MFGB leaders who had urged moderation and caution. He absorbed the lesson of the 1924 negotiations – there was an urgent need to improve the Federation's bargaining power. In June he wrote a major article entitled 'Towards a New Policy: Trade Unionism at the Cross Roads' for *Labour Monthly*. He began by criticising the lack of unity within the trade union movement, and urged reorganisation of the union structure along industrial unionist lines suggested before the war. Cook proposed the formation of 'a united front' by giving power to the General Council of the TUC to organise a co-ordinated fight on the question of wages and hours:

> Upon these questions we can unite together and work, and thus prove to the workers that we are thinking not according to our trade and occupation, but thinking as members of the great working class.
>
> The General Council should at once draft out a scheme ready for the next TUC; otherwise that meeting will be a farce, where we will pass resolutions that we never intend to carry out – that, in fact, we have not the machinery to carry out. . .

Cook also alluded to his long-term objectives, and again the syndicalist node to his philosophy showed through: 'The problems we have to face are changing. New problems demand new methods and new machinery to face them. Therefore, while fighting for wages and hours, our ultimate aim must be control of the industries we work in, in the interest of the whole of the community.' Finally Cook urged that the mistakes of 1921 must not be repeated: 'The divisions between us must cease. . . that slogan "an injury to one is an injury to all" must be made real and live.'

Cook pursued the attainment of an industrial alliance through two avenues. At the Hull TUC in September he succeeded in persuading Congress to give power to the General Council to organise sympathetic action and support during disputes. Cook also attempted to deal directly with other union secretaries amd executives. The economic condition of the coal industry towards the end of 1924 gave greater urgency to Cook's desire for strengthening the MFGB's position. What Dr Kirby has termed 'the realities of the long-term market situation' reasserted themselves, and from September onwards an increasing number of collieries operated at a loss. Wages drifted downwards under the wages:profits ratio scheme established in 1921, and unemployment and short-time working rose sharply. At the Labour Party Annual Conference in October Cook seconded a resolution calling for nationalisation of the mines; but all hope of nationalisation was chimerical. The miners realised that the collapse of the coal trade would spark demands for wage reductions and even longer hours. Cook's statements expressed apprehension, not eased by the Mining Association's invitation to the MFGB to discuss the industry's problems and possible remedies. Writing in *The Mineworker* at the end of the year, Cook predicted that 'The Miners' Federation is to be tested': 'What will 1925 bring forth? It cannot get worse, says the suffering miner, therefore we must hope for improvement. Don't be too sure, fellow workers, it can and will get worse unless we watch very carefully every move.' For Arthur Cook 1924 had been another year of immense personal transition. He found himself in a unique and difficult position: he was the MFGB's only full-time official, based in London and separated from his roots; he was forty-one years old at the end of the year, while the other MFGB national leaders were in their sixties and were full-time officials in various districts. Unlike them and the vast majority of other national union leaders, Cook was a Marxist with a reputation for political intemperance. But he was a revolutionary on the retreat. In the months ahead Cook was obliged to co-ordinate the MFGB's resistance to the almost inevitable attack on its members' conditions, and indeed on the Federation itself. In the mobilisation of the miners' fighting capabilities Cook was to play a vital role: throughout 1925 his influence and notoriety mushroomed as his campaign of public meetings throughout the British coalfields captured the attention of the nation and gained him the admiration and respect of the mining communities.

4   Cook's campaign

Speaking at Cannock on Sunday 11 January 1925, Cook told his
audience that it was time to cease camouflaging the situation;
whether they liked it or not, the miners were face to face with
the most serious crisis in the history of the MFGB. But the
Federation's attitude was clear – wages could not be reduced
and the hours of work could not be extended. Cook predicted
'we are in for a battle'. This was one of the first in a series of
weekend meetings designed to inform and prepare the mining
communities for the struggle anticipated by Cook. It was during
'Cook's Campaign', as Robin Page Arnot termed it, that his
oratorical powers were given full expression. The effect was
remarkable. A meeting addressed by Cook became a major social
event in the miners' calendar. Attendances were difficult to estimate accurately, but reports of crowds around 80,000 were not
unknown. In what was to be a rehearsal for his even more spectacular performance during the 1926 lock-out, Cook made a
major contribution to the rejuvenation of the miners' resolve,
spirit and strength. If he had accepted the customary fees for
addressing these meetings Cook would have become financially
secure, but he astonished other national Labour leaders by rejecting payment, as indeed he had done throughout his career. In
fact, other trade union officials and Labour politicians were usually sceptical, contemptuous or openly critical of Cook's campaign. But the miners loved it. Cook became the focal point and
spearhead of their struggle to avoid starvation wages. His campaign became of enormous importance to the MFGB's collective
will-power. Cook's speeches did not cause or even promote the

battles of 1925 and 1926 (although newspapers, coalowners and government ministers were happy to claim otherwise), but they certainly added an extra dimension of dynamism, fervour and emotion. Cook became the miners' hero.

It is not easy to understand fully how Cook achieved his charasmatic rapport with his audiences. His speeches were performances. In them humour was very important, emotion more so. Oratorical technique and platform behaviour were crucial. A recording of Cook's voice, made in the middle of the 1926 dispute, reveals something of the emotion and pulpit-method in Cook's South Wales accent with its West Country undertone. But this prepared speech lacks the fire and spontaneity one imagines existed in his unrehearsed open-air performances in front of large, responsive audiences. Those who heard Cook speak never lost the memory; from Scotland to Somerset there exists a rapidly dwindling number of veterans who can recall a visit by A. J. Cook to their district. They, too, find it difficult to articulate the reasons why his speeches were so special, and why he gained so much devotion from the miners and their families. But the fondness of their memories is unmistakable. Arthur Horner shared speaking platforms with Cook on scores of occasions, and it took that astute man some time to work out his answer to the riddle of Cook's special appeal:

> I would made a good, logical speech, and the audience would listen quietly, but without any wild enthusiasm.
>
> Then Cook would take the platform. Often he was tired, hoarse and sometimes almost inarticulate. But he would electrify the meeting. They would applaud and nod their heads in agreement when he said the most obvious things. For a long time I was puzzled, and then one night I realized why it was. I was speaking *to* the meeting. Cook was speaking *for* the meeting. He was expressing the thoughts of his audience, I was trying to persuade them. He was the burning expression of their anger at the iniquities which they were suffering.

It was the sort of demogogic appeal which in unscrupulous hands would be dangerous, the sort of appeal that a dictator might have, but Cook was utterly honest and selfless.[1]

Perhaps Cook himself offered a clue to his success when he pointed out that he said in his speeches what the ordinary miner could not say for fear of victimisation and dismissal. Further evidence of Cook's speaking technique is provided by Idris Cox, the South Wales Communist leader, who must have heard Cook on many occasions: 'He was a marvellous orator, he didn't need notes for his speeches, he came to the meeting, he sensed the temper of the meeting, the emotions of the people, he could speak in simple homely words, and he could rouse them to tremendous things.'[2] Cook's platform style was unique. Photographs show his scorn for traditional, respectable, speaking mannerisms. In a mixture of humour and identification with the ordinary miner, Cook took off his jacket, tie, collar and hat. In crowded halls, or in fields or sports grounds, and lacking any sound amplification, Cook would move round the platform, making the same point to different sections of the crowd. Jokes and sayings were no doubt relayed to those who could not hear. Laughter, applause and cheering reverberated through the audience. The moments of quiet emotion must have been scintillating. Robin Page Arnot, who worked closely with Cook throughout 1924-6 and heard him speak to large crowds on many occasions, concluded that

> His speeches were not so much pragmatic as revivalist. He put forward not so much a policy as a recital of grievances. He could tell of the hard lot of the colliers, for he himself had suffered it, and suffered more because of his protests: and in telling of it he roused the miners to mend or end it. He came to be a mirror of the coalfields, to reflect the mood of the colliers, to voice what had been brooded over underground for a couple of generations. The

effect was that soon a greater trust was reposed in him than had ever before been confided in any miners' leader. Audiences greater than ever gathered to Keir Hardie came to hear A. J. Cook. They hung upon his words, and when what they had obscurely felt was so openly spoken, they ceased to trouble over niceties of policy.[3]

The fundamentally emotional appeal of Cook's speaking must not be underestimated. It is essentially true that his rapport with the miners was 'not cerebral but visceral'.[4] But equally we must not forget that Cook was saying *something*, not merely precipitating or pandering to emotions. Certainly he laced his talk with dreams, those of revolutionary changes, of justice, of decent living standards and safer working conditions; he was also an entertainer, and one imagines that many people went to his meetings with less interest in what he was going to say than in the way he said it. But Cook also tried to educate and inform his audiences. Press reports of his meetings reveal that he was careful to bring the rank and file up to date with national developments and frequently aired problems over policies. Just as Cook was not simply an agitator, so it is true that he was not merely the 'Billy Sunday of the labour movement'.

The effect of his speeches was immediate: the Mining Association complained that his campaign was 'likely to create an atmosphere highly unfavourable to reasonable discussion' and arouse hostility to proposals the coalowners might make. But there was no possibility that the miners, Cook or no Cook, would be anything other than hostile to the remedies the employers envisaged for the industry's severe problems. Cook challenged the owners to explore alternative solutions to those difficulties – cut wasteful expenditure; improve efficiency in production, organisation, financing and distribution; and to make better use of by-products. This approach was central to the MFGB's contention that a reduction in production costs could be achieved without reducing wages or lengthening the working day. Another vital strand in the Federation's policy, and one for which Arthur Cook was mainly responsible, was the achievement of an industrial alliance with other unions. Writing in the *Daily Herald* as early as 5 January 1925, Cook had appealed to dockers and railwaymen 'to help us improve our position'. Towards the end of January the MFGB Executive decided to initiate an alliance with the engineers, NUR, ASLEF and TGWU for 'mutual support to our respective memberships at times of necessity'. Cook was determined that such an alliance would gel: he was not prepared to discuss the possibility of a miners' dispute without such support. His speeches invariably included the message 'there will be no miners' strike alone'.

In the early weeks of 1925 the coalowners and MFGB officials met on several occasions and shadow-boxed. Cook was busy producing and presenting a wealth of statistical evidence supporting the MFGB's line of argument, but he was under no illusions. He informed a MFGB conference at the end of February: 'We need not only wisdom, but I think courage, as well as caution, to meet the position. We represent one-tenth of the population. We want reorganization nationally and internationally, and if we are honest we will put down a programme and prepare machinery to put it into operation.'[5] Cook continued to prepare the ground for an industrial alliance, and in his weekend speeches he tended to present an optimistic picture of a united trade union movement – a message designed to strengthen the morale of the rank and file and warn the coalowners. Such talk also put pressure on any reluctant railway or transport union leader. As one contemporary observed, Cook tended to 'copy the methods of the modern advertiser by first popularizing the thing he wished to put over'.[6] But such tactics alarmed and angered many national union officials, who were frightened that Cook's activities were creating a situation which left them little room for manoeuvre. Cook's impact on public opinion was increased in mid-March with the launch of another left-wing newspaper, the *Sunday Worker*. Although the paper was Communist-financed, Cook was a member of the founding committee, and from its inception it was a major instrument in his campaign. He was a constant contributor, with an article on the front page usually accompanied by a recent photograph of him on the back. The first issue was dominated by his article 'Will Cook let us down?':

> I can hear the voices of the suffering men and women in the coalfields – will Cook let us down? Will he be true to his class, or will he forget us in his office in London? Will he fight on our behalf to ensure safety in the mines, and economic security for our families?
>
> Comrades in the mines, I welcome your enquiries, and I hope to retain your confidence. My only hope of success, however, is in the support on an active and intelligent membership of the Federation.[7]

What Page Arnot described as 'mutual long-range shelling with statistics' continued between the Mining Association and the MFGB. At the end of March Cook told his audience in Tredegar that 'a struggle is inevitable', and that the battle would be 'to keep what they had got'. He repeated his old dictum from *The Miners' Next Step*, that the miners could only gain what they were strong enough to win and retain, and he reasserted his stance that he would never lead the miners out alone.

Cook's call for united trade union organisation became more urgent, and he did not seem bothered whether an alliance was formed under the auspices of the TUC General Council or independently. The need for such strength became even greater when Britain's return to the gold standard at the end of April overvalued the pound sterling and put intolerable pressure on the coal industry's ability to compete in foreign markets. By May Cook had convened a conference involving seven railway, transport and engineering unions. At a MFGB conference later that month he expressed hope that an alliance would be formed, and urged caution and patience in the meantime. He clashed with delegates who wanted immediate action, and replied to criticisms that his conference speeches were a marked contrast to the militancy of his weekend oratory:

> My campaign in many districts has been to help to get the men into the organization. In Scotland there are thousands of non-unionists. There are thousands of non-unionists in South Wales. I think that our men are being convinced and converted to the fact that while we are entitled to a living wage it is our duty to get the organization and machinery to secure it.
>
> . . . one may change his mind as regarding tactics. They say a fool never changes, but experience teaches many things, and it has taught me this: if we are going to fight we must have a machine to fight with.[8]

At the beginning of June the conference of invited unions agreed to form a committee to discuss an alliance and draft a constitution. Cook and Herbert Smith were appointed the MFGB's representatives. Throughout June Cook told the miners that the alliance was taking shape, but time was running out. On 19 June the MFGB Executive reviewed the latest meeting with the coal-owners, at which the employers had intimated their intention to terminate the wages agreement and to seek to return to an eight-hour day. The Executive reacted angrily, informing the Mining Association that 'the workmen will not agree to longer hours or lower wages, but will press for increased wages which shall be commensurate with the increase in the cost of living'. At the end of June negotiations broke down in bitter deadlock. Cook accused the Mining Association of declaring war on the miners. On 1 July the owners' wages offer was announced: it was based on their intention to establish a guaranteed profit, irrespective of wage levels. The national minimum percentage was to be abolished, and the proposed district agreements entailed reductions varying from nine per cent inland to forty per cent in the exporting areas of Scotland, Northumberland and Durham. Two days later a MFGB conference rejected the terms unanimously. For Cook the inevitable conflict seemed very near.

On 10 July the MFGB Executive attended a meeting of the TUC General Council. Cook presented a statement of the miners' case, after which the GC resolved to give them their complete support, and undertake to co-operate wholeheartedly with them in their resistance to the mineowners' proposals. The Council also appointed a Special Industrial Committee (SIC) to keep in constant touch with the miners and recommend action if required. Arthur Cook was overjoyed: 'once again ringing through the industrial areas of Britain – in every mine, workshop and factory – is that blessed word Unity'.

Faced with a major industrial crisis, the government intervened in the coal dispute. On 11 July it announced the appointment of a court of inquiry under the chairmanship of H. P. Macmillan, a former Lord Advocate of Scotland. On the 15th, however, the MFGB annual conference at Scarborough decided to shun an inquiry which had for its object the ascertainment whether wages should be reduced or hours increased. Furthermore, a withdrawal of the owners' proposals was deemed necessary before a resumption of negotiations could occur. The General Council's backing gave the MFGB Executive confidence. They disappeared to the districts while the Macmillan Inquiry proceeded without them. In London, however, Cook appeared more flexible. Apparently he dined with W. A. Lee, Secretary of the Mining Association, on 20 July, and Cook agreed to attempt to get his Executive to undertake negotiations in an 'open' situation but without the owners having to withdraw their proposals. The following day Lee wrote to the MFGB officially broaching such discussions. When Cook replied, however, he asked the Mining Association to withdraw the wages terms before any talks could commence, and confirmed next day that his Executive would not budge from the standpoint. The reason for Cook's apparent *volte-face* is not clear. Either he learnt, as the Cabinet Papers suggest, of the South Wales owners' provocative action in posting notices of their terms, or he was simply told to stick to conference decisions when he contacted Herbert Smith in Yorkshire.[9]

On the morning of the 23rd the four MFGB national officials met the General Council's SIC. The atmosphere of solidarity appears to have been genuine, and members were confident of forcing concessions from the government. The prime minister, Stanley Baldwin, negotiated with the SIC, the coalowners and the MFGB, but with little progress. He rejected the option of a subsidy to enable the maintenance of wages, insisting that the coal industry must 'stand on its own economic foundations'. The MFGB made no concessions: when Baldwin stated that the miners must accept a reduction in wages, Cook ruled any such cut out of the question. On 30 July the whole issue reached a climax. In the *Daily Herald* that morning Cook announced his slogan, 'not a cent off, not a second on'. The previous evening Baldwin and Churchill discussed the possibility of a £10 million subsidy for the coal industry. Baldwin kept this from the MFGB officials when they met on the morning of the 30th, and deadlock continued. According to the miners' leaders, as they informed a Special Conference of Trade Union Executives that afternoon, Baldwin had stated that 'all the workers of this country have got to take reductions in wages to help put industry on its feet'. There are no verbatim records of the Baldwin-MFGB meeting, and the government claimed it had been misrepresented, but the effect on the TUC was perhaps decisive. The conference confirmed arrangements to implement a coal embargo and promised the MFGB financial assistance. The Cabinet, meeting that evening, received the TUC decision and agreed by a majority verdict that 'as between a national strike and the payment of assistance to the mining industry, the latter course was the less disadvantageous'. The following day, Friday 31 July, the government announced its decision to grant a subsidy for nine months and to appoint an inquiry in an effort to find a solution to the industry's problems. The owners' lock-out notices were withdrawn. At 4 p.m. Cook sent a telegram to the MFGB district associations: 'Notices suspended. Work as usual. Cook – Secretary.' The *Daily Herald* labelled this triumph 'Red Friday'. Arthur Cook remarked to Winston Churchill: 'Well, Sir, I am glad we have settled it'; Churchill replied: 'Yes, it is a good job it is over, but you have done it over my blood-stained corpse. I have got to find the money for it now.'[10] This was an historic victory for the trade union movement – the coercion of a Conservative government by the threat of national strike action. And the man with whom the triumph was particularly associated was Arthur Cook, whose energetic leadership had galvanised the miners and encouraged unity within the union executives. Baldwin, meeting the Mining Association on 30 July, is reported to have remarked: 'this is Cook's strike'.[11]

Naturally, reaction to Red Friday was mixed. Elements within the Cabinet, Mining Association, capitalist press and even sections of the Labour Party, were horrified. The coalowners were particularly angry, accusing the government of playing into the hands of the 'extremists' and merely postponing the inevitable day of reckoning. Malcolm Dillon, manager of Lord Londonderry's considerable mining interests in north-east England, informed his lordship of a meeting of regional coalowners where it was believed that the Cabinet had not been prepared to deal with a national stoppage, and were 'content to hand over the reins of government to Mr Cook and his colleagues'.[12] The *Daily Mail's* assessment was similar: 'It has been a trial of strength between Mr A. J. Cook and Mr Baldwin, and so far Mr Cook has prevailed. He is the man who has put this country on her back.' In the House of Commons, Lloyd George taunted that the Conservatives had been 'herded into the Red Lobby. The hand that directs them will be the hand of the Patronage Secretary to the Treasury, but the voice that compels them is the voice of Mr Cook.' Even Ramsay MacDonald condemned the government for surrendering 'the appearance of victory to the very forces that sane, well-considered, thoroughly well-examined socialism feels to be probably its greatest enemy'.[13]

The left wing of the Labour movement greeted Red Friday with a mixture of joy and realistic sobriety. The miners kept their feet on the ground: Red Friday has been a triumph for the MFGB and the strategy of which Cook had been the leading advocate. But the Federation leaders, like the coalowners, recognised that Red Friday was only a postponement. The following day Cook and Smith addressed a mass meeting in Renishaw Park, near Chesterfield; Cook's message was clear: 'The fight is only just beginning. An armistice has been declared.' Characteristically, however, to such realism was added the claim that 'the issues during the next nine months were far greater than a mere wage issue. They had got to concentrate on their interests in the industry. It was theirs – it was going to be theirs.'[14] Writing in *Workers' Weekly*, Cook stated that 'this is the first round. Let us prepare for the final struggle.' Indeed, he showed a keen awareness that the expiration of the nine-month subsidy would be followed by renewal of conflict if miners' living standards were to be maintained. He was anxious to use that time to consolidate the MFGB's strategic position. His policy was built on three principles. Firstly, his fundamental opposition to the coalowners' intentions, on economic, political and humanitarian grounds. Secondly, he remained convinced that the miners should not enter a struggle without the support of the TUC. Finally, he was anxious that the MFGB and TUC should prepare machinery for meeting the crisis that loomed – this involved plans for implementing a successful general stoppage should such action prove necessary. Cook's weekend speeches retained their emotional appeal and references to revolutionary changes, but his central message was unambiguous and hard-headed – unity and strength were essential in the months ahead.

The four parties in the mining dispute – MFGB, Mining Association, government and TUC – viewed the nine months, and what was to follow, differently. The miners and the coalowners saw conflict as inevitable. They adopted entrenched positions; the MFGB was desperate to convince the Commission of Inquiry and the government that lowering wages was neither just nor an effective long-term solution, and that far-reaching reorganisation of the industry would obviate a reduction in wage rates. The coalowners denied the relevance of reorganisation, and stuck rigidly to their demands for lower wages and longer hours. The government hoped the problem would somehow go away, or that an Inquiry would come up with a formula acceptable to both sides. But the government also prepared for conflict, and in August resolved to perfect counter-strike machinery which had not been ready in July. By the end of February 1926 the structure was virtually complete. The TUC, like the Cabinet, held hopes that the Inquiry would provide a basis for agreement. In August the General Council decided to retain the SIC in order to 'apply itself to the task of devising ways and means of consolidating resistance of the trade union movement should the attack be renewed'. In the ensuing months, however, the SIC, in contrast to the government, adopted what Professor Crook described as a stance of 'studied unpreparedness'. The General Council did not discuss policy until the termination of the coal subsidy and the commencement of the mining lock-out was almost upon them, leaving such business to its SIC. The SIC,

however, made few plans for a struggle. In September the com-
mittee underwent a small but important change of personnel –
Arthur Pugh, the moderate leader of the Iron and Steelworkers'
Union, replaced the left-winger Swales as chairman, and J. H.
Thomas replaced the more radical NUR leader Marchbank.
Despite promptings from the TUC Secretary Walter Citrine, the
SIC failed to establish contingency plans for industrial action;
moreover, it failed to arm the General Council with a policy.
Ernest Bevin, a member of the GC but not the SIC, felt so
ignorant of events as late as April 1926 that he contacted Arthur
Cook in the hope of enlightenment. A week before the lock-out
Pugh confessed that the SIC had no policy with which to conduct
negotiations.

The SIC's reluctance to prepare was based on a complex
mixture of moderation, defeatism and realism, but above all *fear:*
fear of losing, fear of winning, fear of bloodshed, fear of unleashing
forces that union leaders could not control. Most of these men
were not consciously traitorous, but they lacked moral fibre. As
in 1921, the TUC leadership kept its attitudes, inhibitions and
true intentions from the MFGB. The SIC as a whole did not state
its opposition to a general strike clearly and openly. Aware of
the social justice of the MFGB's policy, the union leaders maintained public support for the miners. They did so in the hope
that the Royal Commission would produce a solution. When
this failed to happen the SIC attempted to extricate itself belatedly
from the MFGB's brotherly embrace. The SIC did not succeed,
however, and dragged the TUC General Council into a battle
they had no appetite for and hence no hope of winning.

The MFGB and SIC agreed that policy-formulation would be
futile until the Royal Commission of Inquiry reported. The miners
felt no need to debate policy, assuming the TUC's 1925 commitments to them still applied. Arthur Cook, meanwhile, conducted
his own preparations; he embarked on a new round of weekend

meetings despite signs that he was feeling the strain of such hectic activity. During his visits to the coalfields Cook often expressed exaggerated threats and unrealistic ambitions. As earlier, however, his speeches had important functions – to improve the strength of the MFGB by increasing union membership, to keep the need for united trade union action in high profile, and to recommend that preparations be made for battle. Unfortunately the insurrectionary rhetoric that Cook threw into his talk tended to capture the headlines and overshadow more practical aspects of his message. For example, in his speech to miners in Mansfield an important point was swamped by statements which were as provocative as they were unrealistic:

> Next May we shall be faced with the greatest struggle we have ever known, and we are preparing for it. We shall prepare the machine and prepare a commissariat department. I am going to get a fund, if I can, in London that will buy grub, so that when the struggle comes, and indeed before it comes, we shall have the grub distributed in the homes of our people. I don't care a hang for any government or army or navy. They can come along with their bayonets. Bayonets don't cut coal. We have already beaten, not only the employers, but the strongest government in modern time. . . Let me warn the government not to tempt the army and navy too much. They are our own lads. I have enough faith in them to know that they will not turn against their own people. Many of them joined the forces because they were out of work.[15]

Cook's belief in the importance of organised food supplies for strikers' families was extremely relevant, and echoed his role in the Cambrian dispute of 1910-11. But his appeal to the working-class loyalties of the army, also reminiscent of earlier militant offensives, frightened many Labour leaders whose support the MFGB was seeking. Some, like Bromley of the SIC, saw through Cook's oratory and appreciated that 'in a battle with the employers one said anything' to strengthen resistance and improve morale. But others, and his enemies in particular, seemed to take Cook's coalfield utterances at face value, and claimed his comments represented MFGB policy. This in turn caused some friction within the Federation, and there were a few right-wing miners' leaders who publicly dissociated themselves from Cook's views and tried to muzzle him. It is certainly possible to argue, then, that Cook's attempts to promote unity within the rank and file was done at some cost, and his speeches were a double-edged sword. But no-one doubted Cook's sincerity and his burning desire to protect the miners; and at least he was doing *something* rather than wait until the crisis arrived.

By the end of August Cook was calling for activation of the 'independent' industrial alliance which was incomplete before Red Friday. This was a thinly-disguised attempt to ginger up the TUC General Council, and at the Scarborough TUC in September he spoke in favour of a motion to vest the GC with powers to call a strike by any affiliated union to assist another union, including the authority to enlist the help of the Co-operative Society to distribute food to strikers. His speech was a more restrained version of his Sunday message:

> Be realists, my friends, realize that it is only power that counts. . . if they were going to win salvation for the working people it would only be by a united voice and united action. . .
>
> Surely we have arrived at a stage when the trade union movement, instead of considering the old method of doling out strike pay, should link up with the Co-operative Movement, should have a commissariat department.[16]

It was during this debate that Cook made his famous reference to the extra tin of salmon his mother-in-law had been putting aside each week in preparation for strike. This was ridiculed by J. H. Thomas, who exclaimed: 'By God! A British revolution based on a tin of salmon.'[17] In fact Cook's speech was a logical attempt to promote the organisation necessary for a successful struggle. But few other TUC leaders wanted to consider such a confrontation, let alone prepare for it. The proposal was referred to the GC for further discussion, and there it was ignored. It seemed that for those who feared a fight, self-emasculation was an important strategy.

Also in September the government announced that the four-man Royal Commission would be chaired by Sir Herbert Samuel, a former Liberal Home Secretary. Cook was not impressed: 'Commissions will not settle the problem of today. Commissions may sit as long as they like, but there is no solution for the miners under the capitalist system. The issue is one of bread and cheese.' Before the Commission began its investigations, however, the pressure of constant over-work at last told on Arthur Cook's health. The MFGB conference on 8 October was informed that he was suffering from 'very severe overstrain', bronchitis and abscessed gums, and Herbert Smith appealed to delegates not to keep writing to Cook asking him to made speeches. But Cook was soon back in action, telling his audiences that he was not trying to cause a revolution, claiming: 'I have never entered a struggle unless it was necessary'; he insisted that 'the real solution of the coalmining industry must be found outside long hours and low wages', and that 'there could be no peace in the mining industry without far-reaching reforms. That meant war. It was time J. H. Thomas got hold of that.' Cook's campaign made him an obvious target for those in the government, Mining Association and the Conservative-owned press who opposed the MFGB. But his attempts to construct a picture of a trade union movement fully supporting the miners also alarmed moderate leaders who were contemplating avenues of escape from conflict. Cook prophesied that the coming struggle would prompt the emergence of 'a new trinity – a linking up of the miners' cause with the political, industrial and co-operative movements. The co-operative movement would be the victualling movement for the fighting forces of labour.'[18] But Ramsay MacDonald was aghast at such a suggestion, while the Co-operative Society was equally horrified by the role Cook had forecast for it. Meanwhile, it was Cook's public arguments with J. H. Thomas which symbolised – or perhaps caricatured – the strains within the MFGB-TUC relationship. Cook's speaking venues ceased to be confined to mining areas, and his audiences must have contained large numbers of railwaymen and transport workers. His appeal for joint action bypassed union leaders and reached the rank and file directly. In prophesying a general strike he was prepared to castigate Thomas openly for his moderation. Cook's tactics did not go down well with TUC leaders: at a meeting of the SIC in January 1926 much time was devoted to criticism of Cook. Thomas was particularly bitter, and was supported by Ben Tillett who complained about the MFGB Secretary 'running down his own colleagues who might be as sincere'.[19] Thomas then wrote an article in the *Daily Herald* accusing Cook of 'childish outbursts' and ruining the MFGB's case; Cook, he said, has 'yet to learn the elemental principles of leadership'. Cook replied in the *Sunday Worker*:

> It is true I do not possess a dress suit, and I do not attend dinners and banquets given by enemies of the working classes and make alleged witty after-dinner speeches there.
>
> Thomas may think that comes within the province of a trade union leader, but if it is one of the 'elemental principles of leadership', I am not going to adopt it.
>
> Thomas is giving vent to his personal spite because I have remained true to the cause of the workers. Along with other noble lords, dukes and gentlemen, he has long wished me in a very warm place.[20]

No doubt Cook's motives for such open bickering were honest, but it was hardly wise at a time when the MFGB was so dependent on the TUC leadership for support. The Federation leadership did not trust Thomas – they were well aware of his role in 1921 – but most kept silent. Cook, however, indulged in an undignified slanging match which did little to foster the spirit of unity he was so keen to achieve. On the other hand, fear of being 'sold out' loomed large in Cook's nightmares, and his verbal attacks were probably designed to neutralise Thomas's influence. If so, they failed. A more comradely attitude towards Thomas and other important moderates like Pugh may have paid better dividends, but such hypocritical posturing was not in the character of men like Cook and Smith.

The MFGB's attempts to foster a formal industrial alliance independent of the TUC failed at the end of 1925. For Cook, the Federation's prime mover in this initiative, and the man whose presence in London made him the linchpin of the organisational work involved, this failure was a serious blow. The miners' hopes of assistance now lay once more with the General Council and its SIC. But at their meeting on 29 January 1926 the members of the SIC attempted to retreat from collision with the government: they rejected a proposal to draw up contingency plans for united action. Thomas led an attack on the assumption that the SIC should remain rigidly loyal to the MFGB's refusal to contemplate longer hours or lower wages, and he dismissed the miners' (and particularly Cook's) contention that a repetition of Red Friday was possible. Three weeks later the SIC met MFGB representatives, and the miners presented their policy and strategy – the maintenance of the 1925 position, plus the need for far-reaching reorganisation of the industry. They recognised that large-scale closure in collieries in exporting districts was inevitable – at a later meeting Smith and Cook used the figure of 200,000 men laid off – but felt this was preferable to lower wages as long as those men received unemployment benefit. The SIC did not commit itself to a policy until the Royal Commission had reported, but it *did* publicly reaffirm its support for the MFGB's cardinal principles of no wage reduction, no lengthening of hours, and national agreements. Phillips has observed that this declaration was out of line with the SIC's previous mentality, and suggests it was made 'almost as an afterthought'.[21] Nevertheless, it was a crucial statement. It is significant that Thomas was absent from this meeting, and at the next session of the SIC-MFGB talks he made strenuous efforts to undo the damage. He ran into a resolute and tetchy Arthur Cook, however, who reminded him that the SIC declaration of support had already been given to the newspapers. Thomas, supported by Pugh and Citrine, persisted: 'They did not want to be too definite. . . they did not want to say anything which might afterwards give the appearance of climbing down.' But Cook protested that 'the three same issues were involved last year. They ought to show a little guts in meeting the situation.'[22] The SIC eventually decided to confirm their commitment to the MFGB's stance, and Thomas was forced to admit defeat. As Lovell has written, the SIC's 'ability to revise its policy in the light of the Royal Commission's recommendations was thus impaired. The miners had won a major tactical victory.'[23] But it was a triumph which ultimately backfired on the MFGB.

The Samuel Report was published on 10 March. It agreed with many of the MFGB's suggestions for improving the industry and recommended national wage agreements and the maintenance of the seven-hour day. But the Commission also concluded that immediate wage reductions were necessary in preference to large-scale colliery closures. Arthur Cook's immediate reaction – 'it gives us threequarters, and we can't accept it' – became MFGB policy. With hindsight, a retreat on the wages question might have saved a greal deal of suffering and paved the way for constructive attempts to improve the industry's structure. But Cook was bound by the Federation's conference and ballot decisions. In any event, the coalowners were not prepared to negotiate along avenues indicated by the Report; in a secret memorandum to the Cabinet they reiterated their rejection of any reorganisation, and concluded that 'no practicable solution of the coal problem can be reached' without increasing the length of the working day.

The MFGB officials met the SIC the day after the Report's publication; Herbert Smith was flexible, and while Cook was prepared to highlight the 'good points' in the Commission's findings, he predicted that the owners were likely to press for huge wage reductions. In fact Cook, despite the image of intransigence and unthinking adherence to slogans which surrounds him, was far more subtle than his President. Cook was prepared to explore the possibility of a compromise, and there is evidence that he was willing to accept reductions in the wages of higher-paid men in return for immediate reorganisation. However, he also believed a general strike would be necessary to force even this from the government. At a MFGB conference on 12 March Cook advised delegates not to reject the Samuel Report outright, so as not to jeopardise the support of the TUC. He was aware of the need to appear reasonable, but he also reaffirmed his opposition to wage reductions:

> I am of the opinion we have got the biggest fight of our lives in front of us, but we cannot fight alone. . . We stand where we stood before. . . Can we say any more? But for the purpose of tactics let us get the minds of the owners and the government, let us keep to the tactics of last year. I think we started right last year. Let us start right now, and I think we shall win.

The SIC, however, was eager to avoid 'the tactics of last year'. Thomas welcomed the Samuel Report as a 'wonderful document', but Cook quashed suggestions that the MFGB should accept the Report in full as 'very previous'; the miners wanted to see what the government had to offer.

Baldwin accepted the Report, but was not prepared to launch a programme of reorganisation immediately. Cook asked him for details of legislative measures which would implement some of the Commission's findings, but the prime minister did not give way. The government refused to discuss reorganisation until the owners and miners had negotiated a wages settlement; the MFGB would not look at wage reductions prior to reorganisation. There was no room for manoeuvre. Meetings between the Mining Association and the MFGB were fruitless; and Cook clashed with Thomas when the railwaymen's leader tried to extricate the SIC from its commitments to the miners. Cook tried to re-establish an optimistic atmosphere:

> they had acted together and done well last year. He thought their tactics were fine this year. The Press had been saying the miners' wages were too low to be reduced. He agreed with Mr Thomas that they could not shout general stoppage every week. But everyone knew this was a postponed event, and everyone was saying there would not be a stoppage.[24]

Cook also resumed weekend meetings, and again he spoke in non-mining areas about the likelihood of a general strike. But the SIC, prompted by Pugh and Thomas in particular, was moving away from its 1925 position of solidarity. Thomas forecast 'a week of bloodshed' if a settlement was not reached; he could see 'a whirlpool into which he was being dragged, without power of responsibility'. When the MFGB officials met the SIC a battle took place over the TUC's position. Cook pointed out that 'the government would accept the owners' interpretation of the Report. . . otherwise the government would have agreed to carry out the Report and not made it conditional on the agreement between the owners and miners'. This logical insight appalled Thomas, who complained that 'there was no hope of a settlement if that was Mr Cook's view'. The SIC and MFGB leaderships were on different strategic wavelengths. On 8 April the SIC refused to endorse the MFGB's three principles. At last it had escaped from its earlier promises.

'That blessed word – unity' was no longer in great evidence, and Arthur Cook began to realise that some retreat would have to be made. The MFGB's allies were reluctant ones; the Federation's opponents were strong. In such circumstances the MFGB Executive – never a monolithic body – began to show signs of internal division: leaders from inland coalfields realised that the coalowners' aims of district agreements and reductions in wages minimal would not be so harmful to their men. Those from the exporting districts, however, saw disaster ahead, and reacted like cornered tigers. Cook, as the only MFGB official with no district responsibilities, viewed the solidarity and unity of the Federation as a personal duty. His awareness of the union's precarious position encouraged him to accept that some wage reductions would be a bitter but necessary price to pay for a settlement followed by reorganisation. Following a meeting with Baldwin on 15 April Cook admitted to the Cabinet Secretary, Thomas Jones, that the industry was 'in the weakest position we have ever been, and while a lot of our chaps won't agree with me, we shall have to have a national minimum not only with pluses above it, but minuses below it'.[25] Cook hoped a meeting between the prime minister, owners and MFGB could 'thrash out the wages issue', but the refusal of the Mining Association to back down over its demands for longer hours and lower wages without reorganisation wrecked his hopes for a compromise.

Publicly Cook remained loyal to the MFGB's three principles. But he was becoming desperate, and his speeches showed it in a characteristic way: he prophesied that a miners' lock-out would mean the end of capitalism; he warned the government that working-class soldiers would not shoot fellow-workers; he also announced that 'if need be, an international strike would be declared'. Kingsley Martin, a socialist intellectual, writing in his diary on 26 April, provided fascinating evidence of Cook's predicament:

> Cook made a most interesting study – worn-out, strung on wires, carried in the rush of a tidal wave, afraid of the struggle, afraid, above all, though, of betraying his cause and showing signs of weakness. He'll break down for certain, but I fear not in time. He's not big enough, and in an awful muddle about everything. Poor devil and poor England. A man more unable to conduct a negotiation I never saw. Many Trade Union leaders are letting the men down, he won't, but he'll lose. And Socialism in England will be right back again.[26]

But Cook wasn't really in a position to 'conduct negotiations'. On the one hand he was bound by MFGB policy to oppose wage reductions, while on the other the miners were confronted by employers and a government who were not prepared to negotiate. A fight or capitulation were the only options. The Mining Association announced ruthless wage terms in several coalfields, including a 3*s* 4*p* cut to 6*s* 11*d* a shift in Northumberland. Such an attack on already low earnings appalled many neutral observers, and stung Cook into greater obduracy. The only hope was another Red Friday. The MFGB informed the SIC that 'the reductions were too serious for the miners to give any consideration to them', and Cook told the TUC leaders that 'they were not far from the time when they would be forced into a conflict' – his terminology implied he did not relish the prospect.

Further meetings between Baldwin, coalowners and miners produced nothing. Cook and Smith repeated their preference for colliery closures and redundancies rather than wage cuts or longer hours. Even the SIC was angered by the employers' vindictiveness, and summoned a TUC conference of union executives at which Cook appealed for sympathy and support: 'we pin our faith in you, and we trust in you to help us solve this very difficult problem. I ask you to trust in us and back us in this struggle for reorganisation and preserving the mining population of five millions from slavery.' That afternoon, 29 April, Cook informed a MFGB special conference that 'the whole of the trade union movement are making every preparation to throw in their lot in the struggle'.

The story of the convoluted events in the few days preceding the General Strike is too lengthy to be completely re-hashed here, but Cook's involvement in these events was at times crucial. The coalowners' lock-out notices were due to expire at midnight on 30 April, and throughout that day miners' leaders, coalowners, government ministers and the SIC were involved in extensive negotiations. At various stages both the MFGB and Mining Association made small concessions, but the gap between them remained profound, and late that night all parties accepted that deadlock could not be removed. The TUC General Council therefore distributed its plans for 'co-ordinated action'; and on the morning of 1 May, with over a million miners locked out, the dispute was brought under the General Council's aegis. Smith agreed that all negotiations would be conducted henceforth by the Council, although the MFGB would have to be consulted. That afternoon a TUC conference of union executives authorised a stoppage.

Negotiations were far from over, however, and the SIC (renamed the Negotiating Committee) approached the government and attempted to find an eleventh-hour settlement. The MFGB's two leading officials had given the TUC grounds for believing the miners might yet settle on terms based on the Samuel Report.

On 27 April Cook, writing in the *Daily Herald,* had declared: 'I am convinced that a settlement can be reached by a straight return to the Commission's proposals, and from them to a discussion on the basis of a national agreement.' Herbert Smith had stated during negotiations on the 30th: 'I am prepared to examine that report from page one to the last page and to stand by the result of the inquiry.' Smith had already stated that he would not simply accept the whole Report, but his ambiguous use of the word 'inquiry' gave TUC leaders the impression he had changed his mind. The MFGB leaders, however, would only consider wage reductions *after* reorganisation measures had been formulated and agreed to by the government – a situation Cook had contemplated privately six weeks earlier. The TUC, however, appeared to negotiate grounds for a settlement on the Report, but without specifying the precondition of reorganisation. On 2 May Cook, who by then was the only miners' leader left in London, discovered the TUC had resumed negotiations with the government. He protested strongly, pointing out that the MFGB had not given an unreserved pledge to accept the Report, and offered his personal opinion that a vague formula – 'that a settlement on the lines of the Report could be obtained within a fortnight' – would not be acceptable. In addition, he urgently recalled his Executive to London. Nevertheless, the TUC Negotiating Committee was prepared to continue discussions on the government's formula, without actually accepting it. The miners formed the impression that the TUC *had* agreed to abandon them in favour of peace based strictly on the Commission's findings. The MFGB leaders were justified in suspecting this, but in fact the TUC-government talks were strained. Attitudes of Cabinet ministers hardened when it became known that instructions from the TUC headquarters mobilising a general strike had been issued. The last straw for the government came near midnight on 2 May when it learnt of the refusal of printers to produce the *Daily Mail's* pro-government editorial. The Cabinet terminated negotiations with the TUC until the strike threat had been withdrawn unconditionally. On the 3rd efforts were made to persuade the MFGB to accede to a new, lower, minimum wage. According to Thomas Jones, Cook repeated his earlier statement that he would consider reductions for higher-paid miners, but regarded the minimum wage as inviolable. Apparently encouraged by Cook, the MFGB Executive decided by twelve votes to six to insist on retention of the existing national minimum. At midnight the General Strike began.

For syndicalists like Arthur Cook, a general strike was the ultimate weapon at the disposal of the trade union movement. In 1918, he had advocated its use to achieve revolutionary change; in 1926 he still talked of revolution in his less restrained moments, but in fact he realised that the General Srike was a spontaneous attempt to protect the miners from degradation. He would have forsaken its use with pleasure in return for economic security and justice for the men he represented. Cook was prepared to make concessions – despite his public stance of unflinching resolve – in response to the MFGB's weak position. As in 1921 he was conscious of the need for a degree of tactical retreat. But in 1926 the MFGB was confronted by employers who wanted more than lower wages and longer hours: the Mining Association was intent on maiming the MFGB and reducing the strength of trade unionism in the coalfields. Cook realised that defeat was a strong possibilty, and that a successful general strike was the miners' only hope. However, his doubts and anxieties were tempered by the exhilaration he felt as a result of the rank and file's remarkable reaction to the stike call: 'Tuesday, May 4th, started with the workers answering the call. What wonderful response! What loyalty!! What solidarity!!! From John O'Groats to Land's End the workers answered the call to arms to defend us, to defend the brave miner in his fight for a living wage.'[27]

The TUC leaders, however, continued to search for a way out of the 'whirlpool' into which they had allowed themselves to be sucked. By the end of the first week they saw nothing ahead but a war of attrition, during which the strike's weaknesses, real and imaginary, would accumulate. Most shared Citrine's view that 'the logical thing is to make the best conditions while our members are solid'. The government, however, refused to negotiate while the General Strike persisted; the TUC, therefore, grasped at the straw provided by Herbert Samuel's intervention. The General Council 'wilfully deceived themselves about the status of Samuel as a negotiator'[28] and surrendered.

Following the outbreak of the General Strike, Samuel contacted J. H. Thomas, who then arranged for Samuel to meet the TUC Negotiating Committee. Samuel based his hopes of a settlement on a formula involving the maintenance of the existing national minimum profits:wages ratio, but with district reductions in basic rates, the establishment of a National Wages Board to supervise the implementation of reorganisation, and the extension of the working day by half-an-hour. These proposals would undoubtedly have been rejected by the Mining Association; in addition, while Cook and Smith had privately stated willingness to accept temporary wage reductions for better-paid men, they were opposed to reductions in basic rates and would have insisted on completely national arrangements. Finally, they would not have entertained the idea of a seven-and-a-half-hour day. The Negotiating Committee, however, while rejecting longer hours, accepted Samuel's other proposals.

The MFGB officials were furious when they discovered the Negotiating Committee had entered into secret talks, and Smith insisted they be included in future discussions. Samuel, meanwhile, had been informed by the government that his initiative could not have official backing. Samuel made this clear to the

TUC leaders, but it is doubtful whether they believed him, or wished to believe him. The MFGB was not informed of Samuel's doubtful credentials. The MFGB officials met Samuel on 10 May, but rejected his formula on the grounds that any reductions in basic wage rates were unacceptable, with or without monitored reorganisation. According to Samuel, Smith led the presentation of the MFGB's case: 'As far as the Miners' Federation is concerned it is Herbert Smith, and not Cook, who is the dominating influence, and his position is up to the present quite immovable.' That evening the MFGB Executive met the General Council. The miners' leaders, Cook in particular, opposed reductions for poorly-paid men, and insisted on national agreements. In addition, the miners were suspicious that once they had yielded on the wages question all the promised efforts to introduce reorganisation would stagnate. Fearing duplicity the miners set their collective jaw. Citrine recorded in his diary:

> Miner after miner got up and, speaking with intensity of feeling, affirmed that the miners could not go back to work on a reduction in wages. Was all this sacrifice to be in vain?
>
> Cook, throwing out his hands imploringly, entreated the General Council: 'Gentlemen, I know the sacrifice you have made. You do not want to bring the miners down. Gentlemen, don't do it. You want your recommendations to be a common policy with us, but this is a hard thing to do.'[29]

All hint of concession disappeared from the MFGB's attitude. The General Council, however, decided to push ahead with a settlement of the General Strike on the Samuel terms. On the 11th Pugh told the miners they could take it or leave it, and that the Samuel formula included the proviso that if the General Strike was terminated the government would instruct the owners to withdraw their notices, allowing the miners to return to work on the 'status quo' while the wage reductions and reorganisation machinery were negotiated. Cook asked what guarantees the General Council had that the government would accept the Samuel terms, and was given an indignant reply by Thomas: 'You may not trust my word, but will you not accept the word of a British gentleman who has been Governor of Palestine?' The MFGB leaders, however, reaffirmed their rejection of the formula and left. The General Council talked on, with Thomas keeping the government informed covertly of developments. Towards the end of the meeting a strategically-timed telephone call from Downing Street encouraged the GC to agree to see Baldwin the next day in order to terminate the General Strike of the Samuel terms.

In fact, of course, Cook's doubt regarding Samuel's authenticity as a government mediator proved justified. Baldwin denied all knowledge of Samuel's role. But the majority of the GC believed they had gone too far to withdraw from a settlement, and proceeded to terminate the strike unconditionally – the coalowners' lock-out notices continued to operate. J. H. Thomas was delighted; indeed he had been the vital lubricant in the peace-making machinery: Samuel wrote to his wife informing her that Thomas 'did splendid work this week'.[30] The miners, not surprisingly, were angry and bitter. They believed they had finally been the victim of a 'culmination of days and days of faint-heartedness', Cook described the predicament the MFGB leadership found itself in: 'Before myself and my colleagues an abyss had opened.'[31]

5   The seven-month lock-out

When the General Strike was terminated the miners were left, as in 1921, to fight alone. Many were accustomed to protracted struggles, but 1921 had been a chilling lesson in the realities of industrial confrontation during a period of high unemployment. Arthur Cook had stated repeatedly that he believed the miners could not win alone; and at the MFGB Executive's meeting on 14 May he offered the same opinion. From the outset he held a realistic – some might say pessimistic – view of the Federation's position. But he did not make his anxieties public; to have done so would have seriously damaged the solidarity and morale of the miners. Furthermore, he was committed to the Federation's policy, and the MFGB Executive was in no mood to wave a white flag in May. The miners' leaders' deep abhorrence to the owners' attacks was sharpened by the bitterness caused by the behaviour of the TUC leadership. This emotional response was buttressed by the MFGB's confidence that the rank and file of the trade union movement would rally to the aid of the miners – that the railway and transport workers would implement a coal embargo, threat of which had produced the government's capitulation on Red Friday. In June Cook published his own account of the General Strike, *The Nine Days*, which was an angry condemnation of the General Council's pusillanimity. But he reflected the mood of the MFGB when he concluded:

> We still continue, believing that the whole rank and file will help us all they can. We appeal for financial help wherever possible, and that comrades will still refuse to handle coal so that we may yet

secure victory for the miners' wives and children who will live to thank the rank and file of the unions of Great Britain.

The miners knew by then that they were involved in a war of attrition. On 14 May Baldwin had offered them terms significantly less favourable than those embodied in the Samuel formula. The prime minister offered an immediate ten per cent reduction in the national minimum wage, a National Wages Board to monitor the fixing of district wages rates and supervise drafting of legislation on colliery amalgamations, a temporary subsidy to ease the impact of wage reductions, and a promise to introduce a longer working day if both the miners and owners requested it. Such terms were more favourable than the Mining Association's demands for compulsory arbitration, longer hours and removal of subsidy, but the government was losing interest on reorganisation and was disengaging itself from involvement in the dispute. This meant, as Dr Kirby has observed, that 'the length of the dispute depended on the miners' will to resist'.[1] The Baldwin proposals were rejected by the MFGB at its conference on 20 May. The terms were also rejected by the coalowners, who objected to the National Wages Board and amalgamations; they demanded an eight-hour day and the cessation of what they termed 'political interference' in the industry's affairs. Confronted by such intransigence Baldwin, supported by Steel-Maitland (Minister for Labour) and Lane-Fox (Minister for Mines), adopted a policy for inaction.

The MFGB was acutely aware of the need for support from the trade union movement if its bargaining position was to be improved. Cook wrote to the railwaymen's unions, NUR and ASLEF, asking them not to handle coal; the MFGB realised it had to create a coal shortage to have any hope of victory. By return of post, Cook's request was refused. The railwaymen's leaders believed they had 'carried out our obligations in conjunction with other unions', and added that due to the coal stoppage they were struggling to achieve re-employment of their members. Such a brusque rejection did not augur well for the miners. The end of May also saw further evidence of the toll events were taking on Arthur Cook's health. Since his election as national secretary Cook had undertaken a massive work-load. In addition to routine office duties, the mining crisis had consigned him to a series of government inquiries, protracted and often bitter negotiations, and frequent MFGB conferences. As the Federation's only full-time national official, this commitment was more than enough: but in addition, of course, Cook imposed upon himself the strain of intensive public speaking and the travel it involved. It is safe to assume that Cook was never able to recuperate fully from his breakdown in 1925. The increasing fatigue and nervous tension told once again before the end of May. Following a meeting back in Porth Cook travelled to Radstock, a small mining town near his birthplace, where he collapsed after speaking. On this occasion he recovered sufficiently to return to London, where his daunting pace of work continued. In the long months ahead Cook's qualities as a trade union leader – energy, courage, moral fibre and realism – were tested to the limit. Part of his brain told Cook that the miners would be beaten; the rest of his body particularly his heart and guts, told him they must fight. And Cook was prepared to devote his remaining strength to the struggle. In the words of Michael Foot, Cook 'seemed to hurl his own physical frame' into the miners' fight.

Together with Herbert Smith, Cook concentrated on efforts to improve the MFGB's strength. Both appealed directly to railway workers for a coal embargo. But the Federation officials were also keen to negotiate, and took part in discrete, unpublicised attempts to find an early settlement. On 31 May Cook, Smith and Richards met Baldwin, Gower (the prime minister's private secretary), Steel-Maitland and Wilson (permanent secretary at the Ministry of Labour). Baldwin informed Thomas Jones: 'I put it to them that "hours" was their way out. If they went on with the strike they would be beaten. I did not move them.' Jones's diary reveals that the prime minister had decided to allow the dispute to continue in the hope that increasing weakness would compel the MFGB to yield.[2]

With no sign of a negotiated settlement, the MFGB launched a weekly newspaper designed to bolster its members' solidarity and morale. *The Miner* immediately became an important factor in Arthur Cook's remarkable relationship with the coalfield communities. The newspaper was an immediate success: its first issue sold 60,000 copies, the second sold 80,000 and the third 110,000. In the first number Cook asked: 'Shall the miners be beaten by starvation? . . . The weapon of the capitalists is starvation. Shall the cry of the child for food break the hearts of Britain's strongest men?' In mid-June he was still prepared to strike an optimistic note: 'we can rely upon our dockers and railwaymen to prevent "black" coal from being landed or transported. We are sure they will not take the side of the owners against us.' But this was desperate wishful-thinking, an echo of Cook's syndicalist belief in the power of the 'triple alliance'. In reality, the attitude of the railway and transport unions prohibited any official action, and Cook and his colleagues placed a naive faith in the potential for spontaneous, unofficial rank and file support in the aftermath of a failed general strike.

In addition to its continued isolation, the MFGB's strength also began to deteriorate internally. Union funds were low if not exhausted; strike payments had shrunk to a trickle. Even the generosity of the Russian workers (who contributed £270,000 in mid-May and promised more) did little to satisfy the needs of over one million miners and their families. The Federation's cause was also hindered by disputes within its leadership. In

Nottinghamshire and Derbyshire leaders such as Frank Hall and George Spencer supplemented Frank Hodges's opposition to official MFGB policy. Hall proposed adoption of a practice, first implemented during the 1893 lock-out, of allowing men to work at pits where pre-lock-out conditions were offered. Frank Varley MP, and influential member of the MFGB Executive, suggested a reduction in the national minimum wage for one year. Frank Hodges, during a speech in Nottingham, claimed that 'the miners would be prepared to accept longer hours in preference to lower wages'. And in Derbyshire Thomas Spencer advocated surrender, for which he was expelled from his position with in the local miners' association.

Under such circumstances the MFGB officials could not have been confident. Moreover, in mid-June they suffered a further blow when the government announced their intention to suspend the Seven Hours Act and legislate for a return to an eight-hour day. The Cabinet had dropped all pretence of impartiality: it had accepted the coalowners' prescription for solution of the industry's economic problems. Perhaps influenced by Hodges, the government had decided that rank and file miners preferred longer hours to lower wages. The government's decision caused deep resentment within the MFGB leadership. This resentment was also tinged with anxiety, for the suspension of the seven-hour day had immense immediate and long-term disadvantages for the Federation. In the short-term it enabled coalowners in the inland districts to offer pre-lock-out wages to miners returning to work. Furthermore, suspension of seven hours threatened the national uniformity – and hence unity – of the MFGB, as only the poorer exporting districts would need to work the full eight hours. The Federation leaders roundly condemned the government's action. Cook declared: 'the prime minister has become the mineowners' advocate', and that 'we are not afraid to call him a liar'. He made it quite clear that the MFGB would never agree to an eight-hour day: 'they may be forced to accept lower wages by sheer starvation, but never longer hours'.[3]

The government's attack on the seven-hour day had three major consequences. Firstly, the MFGB mended their differences with the TUC General Council, which was appalled by Baldwin's policy. Secondly, Arthur Cook commenced another speaking tour of the coalfields in order to stiffen resistance – a campaign which even surpassed his efforts during 1925. And, finally, it persuaded Cook that some means of ending the lock-out with the seven-hour day intact should be found, even at the expense of agreeing to wage reductions.

After the General Strike relations between the MFGB and TUC leadership ranged from bitter to 'rather strained'.[4] TUC conference of executives had been arranged for 25 June, at which post-mortems and bitter recriminations were expected. The GC's riposte to Cook's *The Nine Days* had been drafted by the Negotiating Committee, and their report charged the MFGB with pursuance of 'a policy of mere negation', adherence to 'mere slogans', and other examples of incompetence. The MFGB leaders undoubtedly wished to keep such criticisms private while the dispute persisted, even if they had clear consciences about their performance. Consequently, the Federation appealed succesfully for postponement of the conference. It was agreed that *The Nine Days* would be withdrawn from circulation, while the General Council promised to consider further measures to support the miners. This 'June Pact' angered militants who wished to have the treacheries of the TUC leadership exposed. Cook attracted criticism from the CPGB, which reflected the Communist International's view that he was guilty of covering up the General Council's 'betrayal'.

Cook's new coalfield campaign commenced in the third week of June. At first he devoted a small proportion of his time to propaganda work, and after a day of two's hectic oratory would return to London. But in the absence of official negotiations his days in London grew less frequent, and he proceeded to expend his energies recklessly in a desperate effort to buttress the miners' flagging resistance. Ironically, the summer of 1926 was probably Arthur Cook's finest hour in terms of popularity and often love he evoked from his mining audiences. Undoubtedly his meetings contributed to the persistence of the miners' resolution. Signs of a drift back to work in some hard-pressed mining villages were often averted by a visit from the celebrated MFGB Secretary. Where a return to work had occurred, a rousing speech from Cook usually persuaded miners to renew the struggle. In a very real sense he became an important influence on he miners' collective willpower. Fenner Brockway, an ILP activist in 1926, knew Cook well and possessed both admiration and affection for him; in his autobiography Brockway recalled: 'During the. . . lockout Arthur insisted on foregoing his salary and taking lockout pay and nothing else. He lived in trains, travelling from one coalfiled to another, addressing four or five demonstrations, thousands strong, day after day, wearing out his voice to rough hoarseness and sometimes to absolute speechlessness.'[5] Arthur Horner also recalled Cook's meetings during the lock-out:

> I'd been pacing him in meetings all over the country, this is talking, to keep the crowds – sometimes 80,000 people – in the General Strike – until Cook would arrive, because he knew nothing about (time) tables. He was absolutely undisciplined in that respect, and I often used to wonder – 'what's this man got that I haven't got?' Because people would stand in the rain waiting for him.[6]

George Short recalled a meeting addressed by Cook in Durham:

> I remember on one occasion A. J. Cook was to address a rally of miners at Burnhope, Co. Durham. Miners and their families came from every village in the Derwent and Wear Valleys, in some cases walking 15 to 20 miles. He told the huge gathering the story of the

age-long struggle of the miners against hardship and tragedy, of their rights to live a decent life. He spoke of the way the fight was going in other parts of the country and the efforts being made to win the support of workers in other lands, finally receiving ringing cheers of response to his demand for 'Not a minute on the day, not a penny off the pay'.[7]

These incessant efforts severely impaired Cook's health. He sometimes addressed a dozen meetings in a day, making lengthy speeches at each. His health in general, and his voice in particular, deteriorated rapidly. Yet he seemed to pay little attention to his own welfare. Glyn Evans, a Communist ex-miner working for the Labour Research Department in 1926, has recalled one of Cook's meetings towards the end of the lock-out:

> I remember we went to the Bull-Ring in Birmingham. . . just at the beginning of November and he had been at it every weekend and during the week. . . When we went to Birmingham he was pretty low actually, his voice was hoarse and he was beginning to feel seriously the strain. And I had his notes ready and the chairman announced – the whole place was packed – the chairman announced 'A. J. Cook', and he got up and said, 'Comrades', and you could feel his voice croaking you know, and you could hear the whole audience 'oh, oh'. And after the meeting I had to give him some whisky and rub him down and he was in a terrible state. . .
>
> And we used to go to Doncaster, for example, and then go out to the collieries and he would speak at three or four meetings on a Sunday and then come back Sunday night and be at the office on Monday. It was a terrible strain on him, terrible strain.[8]

For much of the lock-out Cook suffered considerable pain from an old mining injury which flared up after receiving a kick from a demonstrator at Chelmsford. The leg was eventually amputated in 1931, no doubt because Cook refused to visit a doctor for fear of being forced to rest up. It seems that this total commitment and dedication was transmitted to Cook's audiences, who came to regard their National Secretary as a personification of their battle against the coalowners and government. In concluding this brief insight into Cook's oratorical performances during the lock-out, it is revealing to cite Jack Lawson, the Durham miners' leader and the biographer of Herbert Smith:

> Never were such vast crowds seen in the coalfields – perhaps never in Britain – as those which the Miners' General Secretary, Mr A. J. Cook, addressed. From north, south, east, and west came the crowds – far beyond the limits of the immediate district in which he spoke; on foot, by cycle, train and bus the people came; large numbers who were not miners went to swell the crowds. With coat off and sleeves rolled up Mr Cook addressed them. As he proceeded waistcoat would be shed, then collar and tie, until he stood, with shirt neck open, sweeping a vast crowd of people with emotion, as few speakers have ever done. . . Seldom has there been such feeling as swept those crowds. He must have been a superman who could have remained proof against such swirling floods of emotion. That Mr Cook was the subject of great devotion was undeniable. He was a prophet among them. To this day men speak of those gatherings with awe. That the speaker paid for them with his life is beyond doubt.[9]

On the weekend of 19–20 June Cook travelled to Yorkshire, where he spoke at Doncaster and Sheffield, launching scathing attacks on Baldwin, who he dubbed 'the office-boy of the owners'. On the 21st he spoke in Mansfield, where he asked the meeting whether they favoured continuation of the struggle – the crowd voting in favour. Cook's public statements at this juncture, how-ever, were *not* the rigid 'not a second on, not a penny off' stance he had adopted before the collapse of the General Strike. Before May, of course, Cook had mooted privately the possibility of small-scale wage reductions in return for immediate reorganisa-tion. And in late June he was amenable to similar reductions in return for the retention of the seven-hour day. On 25 June he issued the following press statement:

> It is time that the government, instead of continuing this wasteful
> method of conflict between those engaged in a great basic industry,
> should now recognize that it cannot assist the owners by imposing
> terms that will not be acceptable to the men. . . Is it not time, I
> ask, to declare an armistice? Is it not time that the Government
> should withdraw their Bill for longer hours and agree to reopen
> the pits at once on the terms existing in April? Then arrangements
> could be made with the workmen's representatives whereby a settle-
> ment that would give justice to the miners and would secure finality
> without compulsory arbitration. Such a scheme could be worked
> out, while the men are working, in a spirit of fair play.[10]

The government, who had previously complained of Cook's
intransigence noted,[11] but made no official response to, his conciliatory suggestion. Instead ministers encouraged unofficial and
secret attempts to agree a peace formula with the MFGB Secretary. Cook was prepared to go to great lengths to avert an eight
hours Bill, and his search for an alternative settlement led him
into, in the words of Professor Desmarais, 'the worst indiscretion
of his career'.[12] Seebohm Rowntree, the philanthropist, his private
secretary F. D. Stuart, and Walter Layton, editor of *The Economist,*
attempted to mediate in the dispute, and at the end of June
contacted Cook. The ensuing secret negotiations, a sequel (involving Cook and Sir Stephen Demetriadi, chairman of the London
Chamber of Commerce), and their outcome is covered fully in
the Appendix. The Cook-Rowntree talks remained secret until
1928, when Cook was hauled over the coals by some MFGB
leaders for his involvement and his failure to inform the Executive.
The Cook-Demetriadi talks have hitherto remained undis-
covered.

On 2 July Rowntree, Layton and Stuart apparently met Sir
Horace Wilson, permanent secretary at the Ministry of Labour.
Cook, who was in touch with the three intermediaries, verbally

agreed to a proposed peace formula drafted by Rowntree and Layton.[13] According to Rowntree and Stuart's diary of events, Cook was already 'in a state of extreme exhaustion, and one felt in discussing with him that he was almost at the end of his tether. Indeed, it seemed almost cruelty to get him to think.'[14] Nevertheless, Stuart followed Cook to a meeting in Cannock on Saturday 3 July, and persuaded him to sign a document. Stuart assured him the document was secret and for 'the sole purpose of holding up the Eight Hours Bill and securing the opening of negotiations between the Government and the Miners' Federation'. Stuart stated that Rowntree and Layton were confident that if Cook signed, the Eight Hours Bill would be dropped. Cook signed, appending the note: (I am prepared, speaking for myself, on condition that the Government does not proceed with the Hours Bill, to recommend my officials and committee to consider these proposals as a basis for discussion.'[15] The proposals embodied in the document, reproduced in full in the Appendix, were as follows: a joint conference to arrive at an agreed interpretation of the Samuel Report, including the question of the amount of reorganisation to be implemented before any wage reductions became operative; a return to work on pre-lock-out terms; voluntary arbitration on the issue of wage fixation; and the implementation of measures to increase productivity (including the working of double shifts in South Wales). The terms were far more generous than the Mining Association or government proposals, and the emphasis on reorganisation *before* wage reductions made it more favourable than the Samuel formula accepted by the TUC Negotiating Committee. But Cook was prepared, apparently, to sacrifice important principles in return for the retention of the seven-hour day: the double shift system, for example, was despised in South Wales and had been resisted strenuously for decades. In general, however, the terms were far from harsh given the MFGB's deteriorating bargaining position.

During his speech at Cannock Cook asserted:

> the owners believed that if this (Eight Hours) Bill became an Act
> of Parliament, when the proposals were posted at the pit-tops the
> men in the British coalfields would forget their leaders and would
> be prepared to run back on the masters' terms. Next week would
> see the acid test in this struggle. The fight would be won or lost
> during the next fortnight. If the miners stand together, as he believed
> they would, then the British government would be beaten.

On the 4th, however, following his signing of the Rowntree-
Layton proposals, Cook informed his Wigan audience that

> there could not and would not be any negotiation on the question
> of longer hours. The miners would meet the government at any
> time they withdrew that Bill. They would discuss a wages settlement,
> but they wanted it discussed when their men returned to work on
> the 'status quo'. Then they promised they would set up machinery.[16]

This statement reflected the basic policy embodied in the
Rowntree-Layton document. Cook had abandoned the inflexible
'not a penny off, not a second on' position, even if he had not
publicly admitted the need for wage reductions.

Rowntree was disappointed that Cook, in signing the document, had added the proviso 'as a basis for discussion'. Rowntree's
fear that this qualification significantly devalued Cook's signature
was confirmed when he met Steel-Maitland on the 4th. The
minister 'indicated that it would be difficult for him to persuade
the Cabinet to hold up the Bill without something more definite'.[17]
In fact the government had already discussed terms agreed (in
secret) between Lord Wimborne and Tom Richards, and had
decided 'the Hours Bill must be assumed to be law in any further
negotiations'.[18] And on the 5th Steel-Maitland informed
Rowntree: 'Mr Cook's present formula did not go far enough to
justify the government holding up the Bill'.[19] Rowntree and
Layton therefore attempted to introduce Cook to a new proposal

designed to facilitate an eleventh-hour postponement of the Hours Bill. But Cook had already flown to Berlin with the MFGB Treasurer, W. P. Richardson, to collect funds donated by the Russian miners. While Cook was in Germany the Eight Hours Bill became law. With the motive for signing the Rowntree-Layton document now redundant, Cook showed little interest in their proposals. He flirted with Demetriadi's attempt to promote a settlement on the lines of the Samuel Report (i.e. on a seven-hour day), but the advent of the 'Bishops' Proposals' in mid-July ended Cook's involvement in covert, single-handed negotiations.

The introduction of the Eight Hours Act pushed the MFGB's back against a wall. Cook's public message reverted to his slogan of defiance. At his mass meetings he was fortified by the miners' resolve. Cook advocated a return to work on pre-lock-out conditions, and with his colleagues looked once more to the trade union movement for support. On 9 July he declared: 'I feel sure the railwaymen and dockers will not help the government and the employers defeat us by handling coal imported.'[20] On 14 July the MFGB Executive met the General Council, and hoped for sympathetic action. The GC, however, asked the miners to consider a negotiated settlement. The MFGB leaders were not prepared to negotiate on an eight-hour day, and asked the Council to authorise a coal embargo and increased financial assistance. The meeting developed into a bitter argument, with Cook particularly vitriolic. The TUC leaders did not offer help.

Following this blow the MFGB Executive were prepared to consider fresh attempts to restart negotiations on terms which precluded an eight-hour day. On 15 July they met representatives of the Christian Churches, who had contacted the Federation with a view to finding a solution based on the Samuel report. The proposals arrived at in this meeting were for an immediate

resumption of work on pre-lock-out conditions; a national settlement to be reached within four months, with government financial assistance for the interim, reorganisation and wages to be
calculated by the Samuel Commissioners; and the establishment
of a joint board to settle any outstanding disagreements. The
Executive decided to call a special conference to which it would
recommend the Bishops' proposals.

The government, however, rejected the Bishops' Proposals
before the MFGB conference had taken place, on the grounds
that a subsidy could not be given. Furthermore, the MFGB was
not united behind its Executive's recommendation. The South
Wales and Durham districts objected to the churchmen's terms,
as they were contrary to Federation conference policy. At the
special conference on 30 July a distinct difference of opinion was
evident. Cook defended his Executive's actions: 'your Committee
felt that they could not stand idle'. But Arthur Horner, amongst
others, criticised the proposals and the Executive's deviation
from MFGB policy. Cook replied with a tortuous speech in which
he attempted to explain the policy of the Federation leadership.
At the same time he tried to pull the two wings of the union
together – the militants from the exporting districts and the
moderates from the Midlands – by steering a middle course
through the widening gap between them:

> Your Executive thought these proposals. . . would have at least great
> propaganda value, and if turned down by the government and the
> owners our position would be strengthened, and consequently sup-
> port in the country strengthened and supplemented. . .
>
> Whilst our people are willing to struggle on there is a limit to
> physical endurance, and particularly when they see the women and
> children wanting bread. . . That is a determining factor in the strug-
> gle, and this has compelled your leaders to reason whether or not
> to take away every advantage, every opportunity to get an honour-
> able settlement, safeguarding the Federation and protecting our

men from being beaten in this struggle. . .

Are we (the Executive) not right in using any power we may have to open up negotiations? It is because I value the power of this organization, and because I want to keep it intact that I want to see a national agreement with a national minimum. . . As long as the eight hours is there it is a fight for life all the time. I would give this right arm to get it back. . .

I don't like the (Samuel) Report – I hate it – but it is not a question of likes and dislikes. It is a question of determining how strong we are to get what we want. I have to look around at what is happening. . . Unless we can get some means of life in our people then our people will say, is this leadership? Somebody has asked, is it leadership to sit still and drift, drift to disaster? That is not leadership. I say that if this conference believes we can fight another six weeks I will do my best. . . but as long as I am Secretary I ask you as I ask myself to face the facts, and come out of the struggle not demoralised, but to retain confidence in each other and not tell everybody that Labour is dead.[21]

As in 1921, therefore, Cook displayed the ability to recognise weakness and the need to retreat and compromise. He attracted praise from an unlikely source: George Spencer congratulated him for 'one of the most remarkable speeches coming from him that this conference has listened to'. Some delegates, notably those from South Wales, were not so impressed. It is evident that Cook and his old colleagues from the Minority Movement were not agreeing on strategy – a situation which continued for the rest of the lock-out. At the end of the debate, however, it was decided to put the Bishops' Proposals to a ballot of the MFGB districts.

It seems obvious that Cook's advocacy of the proposals, however reluctant, was prompted by the ebbing resistance and increasing deprivation in some coalfields. In Nottinghamshire some 700 men were working underground, while outcropping (collecting coal from the surface) was causing concern. In Derbyshire outcrop working was prevalent and the coalowners were tempting men back to work. In Warwickshire and Staffordshire the position was far worse. By mid-July some 2,500 men were working, and ten days later the figure had leapt to 7,000 out of a total work-force of 22,000. The timing suggests that the Eight Hours Act had enabled local coalowners to offer attractive wage rates. In an effort to stem this breakaway the MFGB sent some of its best speakers – W. H. Mainwaring, Vernon Hartshorn, Stephen Walsh (Lancashire) and, of course, Cook – to the weakened area. Cook's oratory during his weekend visit to Warwickshire on 24-25 July was an unrestrained attack on blacklegging. At Bedworth he said: 'every man who had returned to work was not only a blackleg, but a betrayer of his own children and of the Miners' Federation'. At Nuneaton he called for peaceful picketing to persuade men to come out. In Walsall he asserted: 'if the fight continued they would stop coal coming into the country from abroad. Law or no law, hook or by crook, they were going to stop it.'[22] The agitation had a dramatic impact: by the end of July the number at work had fallen to some 1,600. But the situation was by no means solved, and the drift back to work in the West Midlands soon recommenced.

In the days preceding the district ballot, Cook recommended the Bishops' terms to his audiences. He also claimed that the reorganisation proposals could be carried out within four months and would obviate the need for wage reductions. This view seriously overestimated the scope for rationalisation to counteract the long-term market forces operating against the coal industry, particularly in the exporting areas. Cook's claim was greeted with incredulity within government circles. He realised the Bishops' Proposals were the best available and was anxious that the MFGB district vote should accept them. He must have been dismayed when the ballot produced a wafer-thin majority against the terms. Cook returned to his speaking tour, publicly claiming pleasure in the spirit and determination revealed by the vote. The headlines of the *Sunday Worker* for 15 August proclaimed "NO COMPROMISE! SAYS COOK'. But in South Wales, where the men were virtually solid, he gave vent to his true feelings. He unequivocally recommended compromise, and was prepared to criticise the South Wales decision to reject the Bishops' Proposals. In a speech back in Porth he explained:

> It is not cowardice to face the facts of the situation, and I say that a leader who leads men blindly when he knows different is not only a traitor to himself and his own conscience, but he is betraying the men he is leading. . . I claim that if you knew as much as I do, because I have seen what you have not seen, there is not a man among you but would say, as I today, that you men in Wales made one of the greatest mistakes you ever made by turning down the recommendations of your leaders. . . It was not his duty now to sit still and see the miners drift back to starvation. . . I say 'open the pits next week on the conditions of April, and drop the eight hours, and we will explore the position'.[23]

This speech was both brave and realistic. The South Wales miners, who had most to lose from defeat, remained committed to an intransigent policy. But by 1926 South Wales had established a tradition of solidarity and determination; the MFGB leaders, however, knew that areas such as Nottinghamshire were traditionally weak links in the Federation's defences. The Midlands were the likely source of breakaways, as miners there knew a return to work was possible on relatively generous terms. Arthur Cook, as MFGB Secretary, could not only reflect the opinion of the Rhondda. He had toured Britain's coalfields, witnessing the privations and the vulnerability of the Federation's position. He feared for the survival of the national organisation if a settlement was not achieved quickly. The public's image of Cook was of a revolutionary fanatic committed to the overthrow of capitalism at whatever cost to his members, acting as the dupe of

Communists, and whose emotional outbursts precluded rational argument. But Cook was not the 'inspired idiot' of Beatrice Webb's diary. The events of 1921 had shown that his responsibilities as a trade union leader outweighed his desire for revolutionary change. Conscious of the futility of continued struggle and fearing for the survival of the SWMF, he had recommended retreat. Little was different in 1926: the MFGB was fighting the same kind of defensive battle. As in 1921, Cook saw it as his duty to provide a pragmatic alternative to the 'fight to the finish' advocates.

On 16 August a MFGB special conference assembled to hear reports from the districts. Delegates were divided: Ablett urged negotiation; S. O. Davies asserted 'we can win'. Cook threw his weight behind a compromise settlement. He admitted 'I have never believed the miners could win alone', and in another brave, though disconsolate speech, announced:

> If you want a scapegoat – I am here to be that. If you want somebody to be sacrificed, I am willing to be sacrificed. . . We are now in the 16th week of the struggle. . . can anybody say at the moment that our men are as strong today to fight this battle as they were on the 1st of May? I believe we were right in the things we have demanded, but it is useless to say conditions have not changed since the 1st of May; they have changed to our detriment. There is that Act of Parliament there . . . You know how dangerous it is going to be with this Act, that it cannot be removed until another election takes place, so that it is essential we should have a national agreement. We have got to safeguard these two issues. . . I think that everybody in this conference agrees there is nothing as important as the question of retaining the hours. . .
>
> Our case is just and right, and we shall never succeed until we meet to secure it. . . We have said, work on the 'status quo' for four months, organize the industry, question of royalties, abolition of middlemen, and sales agencies. If these cannot be got voluntarily

or by force, other than forcing the government, then I say let us face the position together. If you say to me, you are wrong, I will admit it if you can prove to me that we can secure something better than these. It seems to me if we sit still, it gradually become a question of district by district, and pit by pit. I have, personally, no quarrel with anybody, but I do think it is better to face this now than in a month's time when we realize we are beaten, and have imposed upon something a lot worse... I ask you to face the position or produce some alternative, or at least prepare some other means to get victory.[24]

Despite criticism from Horner and Bevan, Cook's policy was accepted by a delegate vote of 428-360, and the MFGB leadership was given permission to enter unconditional negotiations with the Mining Asociation.

Those talks broke up acrimoniously, the coalowners making it clear they wanted longer hours, lower wages and district agreements. With no immediate prospect of a negotiated settlement, Cook left once more for the weak spots in the Midlands. His attitude towards blacklegging became more extreme – he claimed he was collecting the names of all those working in the hope that they and their families would be ostracised. In Nottinghamshire and Derbyshire, towards the end of August, Cook's key message was 'Don't stab the Federation in the back', and he advised men to picket in the streets. In three days he addressed approximately fifteen meetings, speaking for at least ninety minutes at each. It is difficult to imagine his physical condition; at Bolsover he was exhausted, and an appeal had to be made to the crowd to allow him to walk quietly to a waiting car. But the impact of his presence was dramatic: one local newspaper reported that 'many men were kept from continuing or going to work', and that 'a considerable amount of feeling has been engendered in the dispute... which up to this time has been absent'.[25]

Following his tour of the East Midlands Cook returned to London, where the MFGB officials met government representatives on 26 August. Baldwin had gone to France on holiday, and Winston Churchill had been placed in charge of coal negotiations. The four miners' officials had already seen Lord Wimborne on the 25th, and he had found them 'rigid, especially on the question of hours'. On the 26th, however, Cook and Richards, at least, were anxious to reach agreement with the government. The temper of the Cabinet had been affected by Cook's weekend speeches, which they interpreted as confirmation of intractibility.[26] Thomas Jones, however, felt that 'Cook and Richards are prepared to yield on wages and hours if they could save their face somehow and secure a national agreement, but I don't see any one of them admitting this to the ministers in the presence of the others.'[27] When the meeting actually took place it was evident that Cook was willing to compromise, although there is no evidence that he was willing to consider accepting an eight-hour day. Herbert Smith, however, relapsed into obduracy on being informed by Churchill that a subsidy had 'long passed out of the sphere of practical politics'. Cook asked the chancellor:

> do you not agree that an honourably negotiated settlement is far better than a termination of struggle by victory or defeat by one side? . . . Is there no hope that now even at this stage the government could get the two sides together so that we could negotiate a national agreement and see first whether there are not some points of agreement rather than getting right up against our disagreements.[28]

Churchill, however, expected the miners to make immediate concessions, and implied that the lock-out was not starving the country of coal and that the MFGB, therefore, could not win. Smith had heard enough and wished to terminate the meeting. Cook, however, remained conciliatory, and stated: 'Now if sacrifices are to be called for in an industry the sacrifices ought to be shared as equally as possible. On hours we say no. On national minimums we feel, as we have pointed out, that some consideration can be given. It is a question that can be discussed.'[29] The MFGB President had the last word, however, and ended the talks with a warning: 'we are not prepared to say at once we will give a reduction of wages to help the employers'. Clearly a major difference of opinion existed between the Federation's two principal officials. Thomas Jones informed Baldwin that:

> it was evident that Cook especially was anxious to get out some such proposals; but Herbert Smith had his foot on Cook's neck. When the meeting was over Cook in unmistakable language told Gower and me what he thought of Smith and he tried to make our joint communiqué to the Press say that the men were prepared to face a reduction in wages. This I had to turn down as it went beyond what took place and would have justified Smith denouncing it.[30]

The relationship between Cook and Smith is not easy to establish. After a wary start the two seem to have developed a mutual respect during their many hours of shared stress. By the middle of the lock-out, however, they seem to have drifted on to different wavelengths. Undoubtedly Cook felt Smith's obstinacy to be impractical and damaging. Smith, however, as MFGB President, was the Federation's chief spokesman, and Cook could not officially or openly dissociate himself from Smith's position. The MFGB special conference had granted the officials unfettered negotiating power, but Smith seems to have grown more stubborn as the miners' bargaining position worsened. One may admire his spirit, but not his wisdom. It is likely that by this time Smith reflected a minority view within the Federation Executive, but as President his position was unchallengeable, and there was no public dissent at his inflexibility. Cook, meanwhile, had embraced a conciliatory, face-saving position: he was only too aware of the drift back to work in some areas; he saw the deteriorating condition of many miners and their families. His nightmares were becoming reality – the MFGB was being ground into defeat, and the survival of the national Federation was at risk. But Cook had no hope – and almost certainly no intention – of usurping his President's role as chief decision-maker. Hampered by Smith's intransigence, Arthur Cook's anxieties grew rapidly.

Despite his fears Cook threw all his remaining reserves of strength into the shoring up of the MFGB's position. At the end of August varying reports put the number at work in Nottinghamshire at 9,500-12,000, out of a total work-force of 36,000. The situation is Warwickshire was also causing great concern, and Cook visited the coalfield during the weekend of 28-29 August. His verbal attacks on blacklegs were intensified, and he also launched bitter rhetoric against the police who protected working miners. A MFGB special conference on 2 September heard further evidence of faltering resistence in the Midlands, and authorised the Executive to negotiate on hours and wages. The following day the MFGB leaders agreed to concede wage reductions.

The MFGB informed the government: 'we are prepared to enter into negotiations for a new national agreement with a view to a reduction in labour costs to meet the immediate necessities of the industry'. The miners' leaders hoped that enough had been sacrificed, and that their third principle – maintenance of a national agreement – would survive. But the Mining Association refused to compromise on that issue. With the Federation in disarray, the coalowners were ruthless in their determination to push home a major attack on the MFGB's strengh and bargaining power.

The Federation officials, particularly Arthur Cook and Tom Richards were now most anxious to reach a settlement with the government which would preserve the national agreement. They also hoped that Churchill, in the absence of Baldwin, would put pressure on the coalowners to make some concessions. William Brace, the veteran South Wales Miners' leader, told Gower on 7 September that:

> I was told by Mr Tom Richards in the strictest confidence that there was a substantial movement in the Miners' Executive in favour of conceding the 14.2 per cent granted to the coal getters as compensation when the hours were reduced from eight to seven, upon condition that the owners would agree to a national agreement upon the 1921 basis and a seven hour day. I gather Smith is against any move but Cook can be counted in favour of going to great lengths for a settlement of the dispute without delay. . . Herbert Smith appears incapable of appreciating what a mess the Federation is in; Cook is much more alive to the danger.[31]

Cook at this time appeared to Beatrice Webb as 'over-wrought – almost to breaking-point', and she believed that 'if it were not for the mule-like obstinacy of Herbert Smith, A. J. Cook would settle on *any* terms.'[32] Cook was not prepared to settle on any terms, of course. But he had resigned himself to major concessions on hours and wages. With his fellow national officials, however, he urged the Cabinet coal committee to persuade the Mining Association to negotiate a national agreement. Meanwhile, he continued to call upon the miners to remain loyal to the Federation: 'on that depends your opportunity to secure a national settlement, so that we may all go back to work together, protected against victimization and with our organization intact'.[33]

On 13 September, however, Evan Williams informed Churchill that the coalowners would not negotiate nationally. The MFGB Executive, with another peace initiative rejected despite its concessions, had a stark choice between total surrender and continued resistance. It chose to fight on, requesting 'the miners in every area to resist the efforts of the coalowners to secure their defeat'. Cook, speaking in Chelsea on the 14th, stated: 'whatever the consequences might be, the miners would not accept or surrender to the terms laid down by the owners. If they were beaten it would be by the imposed terms of starvation... The trade unions should now, at this late stage, impose an embargo on coal and a levy on their members to assist us'. Baldwin returned from Aix-les-Bains on the 15th, and soon made it clear to the MFGB that he was not prepared to coerce the Mining Association on the subject of a national agreement. Cook, meanwhile, asserted that peace was not possible unless under such an agreement: 'the miners will never voluntarily accept district settlements'. On Sunday 19 September he was again in the Midlands. At Longton, near Stoke, he declared: 'I shall raise my voice without fear or favour against considering for one moment going back to the districts and having a settlement district by district.' Later in the day he was in Leicestershire, where he revealed that the Executive was prepared to consider a temporary reduction in wages, a temporary reduction in the minimum, and an 'honourable agreement that would enable all men in their districts to return to work together'. On his return to London he joined his Executive in issuing an indignant reply to Baldwin's offer of district settlements. But the prime minister made it clear that a national agreement was out of the question. On 24 September he informed the House of Commons that the government 'have got pretty well to the end of its powers of mediation'.

Cook spent the following weekend in the Somerset and Forest of Dean coalfields. At Radstock he said: 'I believe in organized retreat. If we have got to retreat and to recommend a compromise, we must do it in a disciplined way.'[34] At Cinderford he stated: 'We will face the position with a view to keeping the coalfields together and the Federation intact, because that is all-important'. Back in London, however, Cook heard Churchill conclude a debate in the Commons on the coal dispute, prior to

the adjournment of the House for a month; the chancellor made
it clear once again that district negotiations were the only hope
of an end to the lock-out. Privately Cook conceded that the
miners would have to suffer wage reductions and longer hours.
Publicly he had admitted the need to retreat. Cook had continued
to hope, however, that 'the government would meet them on
the point of a national agreement'.[35] Churchill's Commons statement destroyed the MFGB's last hope of salvaging anything from
its pre-lock-out position. Furthermore, at a special conference
on the 29th, it was revealed that 81,178 men were working
underground. Of that total, 50,600 were in the Midland Federation, Nottinghamshire and Derbyshire. Herbert Smith
announced that he, Cook and Richardson were flying that night
to Ostend in an effort to persuade the Miners' International to
implement a sympathetic strike. On the 30th, with Tom Richards
in the chair, the conference rejected a South Wales resolution
by Arthur Horner calling for an intensification of the struggle.
Instead it was agreed to call a district vote on the government
proposal for area agreements.

With total defeat staring the miners in the face, Cook's attitude
shifted back toward intransigence. The ruthless policy of both
government and Mining Association provoked bitterness and
renewed resolve. Now there could be no compromise – a settlement meant lower wages, longer hours *and* district agreements.
Cook was desperate, but he was not yet ready to accept total
surrender. However, the MFGB officials' trip to Belgium was
fruitless; the TUC was, yet again, the miners' only hope. In the
Sunday Worker Cook repeated his call to the rank and file trade
unionists to 'urge your leaders to apply a levy and embargo'. On
his return from Ostend Cook travelled to Scotland, where he
stated that the owners' and government's proposals were 'framed
with the definite object of smashing a national agreement and

the Miners' Federation'. At Clydebank he declared:

> We are voting this week on terms that mean surrender. I don't
> know how they will vote. It is not intelligence that will decide. If
> only we had contributions coming in there would be no consider-
> ation of any compromise. It has been forced upon us. It is the labour
> movement, it is the trade unionist movement, that has also forced
> it. The miners leaders may have made mistakes, but one mistake
> we have never made: we have never betrayed the interests of one
> man.[36]

It is revealing that neither Cook nor the MFGB Executive made
any recommendation to the branches in the ballot. It seems
certain that Cook was torn between the unacceptability of the
terms on offer and the suffering and drift back to work in the
coalfields. With hindsight surrender at this point would have
saved a further six weeks of fruitless hardship, but Cook could
not bring himself to advise such a policy, and the result of the
district ballot revealed the miners' courage and determination.
At the MFGB conference on 7 October it was announced that
only the lodges in Derbyshire and Leicestershire had voted in
favour of the government proposals for district settlements. On
a card vote the figures were 737 to 42. This was not an individual
membership ballot, however, and was at odds with the number
of men returning to work. Nevertheless, it was binding on the
conference, which went on to debate another South Wales resolution calling for intensification of the fight, including the withdrawal of safety workers. Cook had to be guided by the result
of the district ballot, but he was in a pessimistic frame of mind:

> What we want is how we can bring pressure to bear on the govern-
> ment to consider our demands. My own answer quite frankly is –
> I cannot see how we can do it. . . as long as I am Secretary I am
> not going to allow you to shut your eyes to the facts we have to
> face at the moment. . . if you adopt the resolution from South

Wales, so far as the safety men are concerned, if you were to withdraw the safety men we would have the blue-jackets, and you would have the soldiers protecting the men at work, and you would have a repetition of 1921, which I hope never to see again. If you do not accept this proposal, then the Executive can sit down to consider the whole proposal again.

These were hardly inspiring words, and after a particularly power-ful and persuasive speech by Aneurin Bevan the South Wales resolution was passed by 589 votes to 199. The resolution laid down that the MFGB 'revert to the status quo conditions'. To achieve this all safetymen were to be withdrawn, an attempt would be made to organise a coal embargo, efforts to stop out-cropping would be inplemented, a TUC levy was to be called for, and propaganda work in the coalfields was to be stepped up. Although Cook was opposed to the withdrawal of safety workers, he had no option but to accept the vote. At the end of the conference he announced: 'I take it everybody will see to it that everything possible is done to keep the men from going to work, and to bring those out who are at work.'

The adoption of the South Wales policy was a desperate act of defiance. But however one may admire the bravery and spirit which lay behind the decision, one must conclude that it had little to do with practicalities. Shirkie, secretary of the safetymen's union, called it 'a gigantic piece of bluff', and claimed that the MFGB had no power to call out safety workers.[37] On past experi-ence, the TUC were unlikely to sanction a coal embargo or a levy. The hope that miners whose families were starving would stop mining or outcropping proved unrealistic. Nevertheless Cook, despite his misgivings, worked strenuously to revive the MFGB's position. In The Miner he called for the imminent Labour Party annual conference to 'sound a clarion call which will rally the whole movement to take active and practical measures, such as an organized levy'. In the Sunday Worker he observed that 'the new policy means a return to the slogan: 'Not a minute on the day, not a penny off the pay'. The men are now driven to use every weapon in their armoury', and he demanded 'concrete measures rather than expression of sympathy' from the labour movement. Cook spent four days in the Nottinghamshire-Derbyshire district rallying support for the continued struggle. He launched scathing attacks on George Spencer, who had negotiated a return to work deal with local coalowners. Cook balked at encouraging the withdrawal of safety workers, however. He stated that such an action was a 'double-edged sword', and that 'I am very anxious that at this juncture the miners shall not take any action which will jeopardize the sympathy, help and support essential to ensure success in the struggle'. At Heanor Cook stated: 'I don't want to destroy. I want to build.'[38] Such statements offended his allies on the left. *The Worker,* the journal of the National Minority Movement, warned Cook that his policy would lose him the confidence of most of his supporters, and urged him to 'Fight, Arthur, Fight like Hell, the men are with you.' Indeed it was the left-wing viewpount which attracted support among MFGB lodges; a district ballot vote to ascertain opinion on the South Wales policy produced a 460,150 to 284,336 vote in favour.

The MFGB Executive met on 15 October to discuss means of implementing the South Wales resolution. Cook was instructed to contact the safetymen's union and the General Council with a view to meeting. The Executive also decided that their future meetings should be held in the coalfields and that the next one would be in Nottinghamshire. Finally the committee made arrangements for greater propaganda efforts. Cook returned to the coalfields. He toured Durham urging the men to remain loyal, and at Ryhope he stated 'they had got to fight because they could not do anything else'. The following day he was in Lancashire, where he addressed several meetings, during which he made the following reference to blacklegging: 'It had got to be stopped. Stopped they must be. Brought out, law or no law.'[39] Such rhetoric seldom had any lasting effect on those who had already gone back to work; miners often responded to Cook's oratory and the anti-scab atmosphere his visits engendered by ceasing work for a few days, only to return when willpower waned once more. The government, nevertheless, was concerned at Cook's ability to slow down or halt the drift back to work. On 18 October the Cabinet met to discuss the MFGB's new policy, and noted that the number of miners at work had fallen by 18,000. Under such circumstances the Cabinet debated whether Cook's statement that blacklegs must be 'brought out, law of no law' constituted a breach of the regulations under the Emergency Powers Act.[40] The Attorney General informed the Cabinet that he had already instructed the Director of Public Prosecutions to 'obtain full and authentic versions of Mr Cook's speeches and to advise him on the question'.[41] In the House of Commons Joynson-Hicks revealed that the police were taking verbatim reports of Cook's speeches, and that the MFGB Secretary had made several inflammatory speeches in recent weeks. But, the Home Secretary stated, 'up to the present I have not seen fit to take proceedings against Mr Cook. . . I have had to realize that he is the admitted leader of a large body of men. A heavy responsibility would rest on me if I were to take away from the Miners' Federation the leader in whom they believe.'[42] The police, meanwhile, had clamped down on miners' public meetings. At Cannock 500 police and thirty mounted police were called in to control any disorder following the Chief Constable's decision to ban a meeting at which Cook was due to speak.

The MFGB's intensification policy proved a failure. The TUC General Council attempted to induce the miners to accept district negotiations. The transport unions informed the Federation that they were unable to organise a coal embargo. On 3 November a TUC conference of executives rejected a compulsory levy on wages, but recommended a voluntary daily contribution of not less than one penny per day. Cook, meanwhile, had continued his propaganda work. During a speech in Pendlebury, Lancashire, he was hoarse and on the point of collapse. His slogan at this time was 'Back to work we go, on the status quo'. At a MFGB special conference on 4 November he seemed unwilling, despite his earlier pessimism, to contemplate total defeat. He was hopeful that the miners could fight on if the voluntary levy was productive. Yet he also agreed that the MFGB Executive should continue to explore means of reaching a settlement, using he offices of the TUC's 'mediation committee'. Two days of fruitless negotiations with the government ensued.

On 7 November Cook delcared: 'I would rather see the organisation broken down and built up again than that we should sign away the conditions our men ought to have.'[43] It is hard to believe that Cook really meant this, however – the survival of the Miners' Federation was of overriding importance to him. Nevertheless it seems Cook was not capable of stomaching the total defeat that was then inevitable. At a MFGB conference which commenced on 10 Novemver it was learnt that 240,000 miners were working. The Executive recommended that 'unfettered' negotiations with the government should take place. But Cook could not swallow this and urged that a full-scale ballot of the membership be taken. The Executive's advice was accepted overwhelmingly, however, and negotiations took place throughout the evening and night of the 11th. The government offered district settlements, a wages to profit ratio on the industry's proceeds to vary between 87:13 and 85:15 and no guarantee against victimisation. On the 12th Cook, Horner and Bevan argued whether an individual ballot should be held, with Bevan claiming the terms were too harsh to be considered. The conference authorised another district branch vote, with the terms being recommended for acceptance.

Apparently Cook hoped for rejection of the terms. The *Sunday Worker* attributed to him a statement: 'my advice to the men is to reject the government's terms', but Cook denied such contravention of Federation policy and the *Sunday Worker* corrected itself. The Communist Party, however, had already distributed leaflets quoting Cook's reported statement. Peter Lee, the Durham miners' leader, claimed the circulars – headed 'Stand by Cook and reject the terms' – heavily influenced voting. Writing after the ballot had taken place but before the result was known, Cook described the proposals as 'abominable'. And the lodges, influenced by left-wing agitation and drawing upon last reserves of determination, rejected the government offer by 460,806 votes (made up from seven districts) to 313,200 (from eleven districts). At this late stage therefore, Cook seems to have aligned himself with the left wing of the large exporting districts who favoured continued resistance – there, after all, was his ideological home. But surely this was a case of Cook's heart ruling his head. Nothing was to be gained from further struggle; the miners were beaten, and surely Cook knew it. The MFGB Executive decided that the district vote was 'born not out of realism but desperation'. The miners' leaders were conscious of their inability to bring increased pressure to bear on the government, while the return to work had become a flood. After much discussion the delegates decided by 502 votes to 286 to authorise the districts to open negotiations with the coalowners.

The seven months' lock-out thus ended. In some coalfields the spirit of resistance remained intact: in South Wales, in particular, the return to work had been minimal. The onset of cold and hunger, however, had quickened the drift back in other areas, particularly within the inland coalfields where most miners had less to lose than the South Wales men. In most districts the eight-hour day was enforced, and in South Wales longer hours were accompanied by lower wages. In the more profitable coal-fields, however, wage rates were comparatively buoyant. In Nottinghamshire, the settlement negotiated by George Spencer and his nascent breakaway union provided for a 4s a week rise. By the end of November all the coalfields were working. Meanwhile the post-mortems and recriminations had begun.

6 'Love to all from one in a lone struggle'

There were no silver linings to the heavy, dark clouds that hung over the coalfields and the career of Arthur Cook after 1926. Conditions varied from district to district, of course, but demoralisation was widespread. Many miners found they had no jobs to return to as many coalowners used the eight-hour day to reduce their labour force while maintaining productions levels. Victimisation was practised widely. Militants were often purged from payrolls. Blacklists were drawn up and circulated among employers; many energetic trade unionists never worked in a pit again after 1926. Following months of existence on meagre lock-out payments and charity, many miners' families were sucked by unemployment, short-time working, debts and low wages into abject poverty.

Cook's immediate response to the miners' defeat was one of defiance. Speaking in Lancashire towards the end of November he claimed:

> The Miners' Federation would never be broken. . . They would begin the struggle again. They were going to wipe out the Eight Hours Bill. From every valley from John O'Groats to Land's End they were going to cover the country by an intensive campaign. They would build up a finer organization and one powerful national miners' union.[1]

In a press statement on 28 November Cook announced:

> I declare publicly, with full knowledge of all that it means, that the Miners' Federation will leave no stone unturned to rebuild its forces, to remove the eight hour day, to establish one union for the miners of Great Britain, and a national agreeement for the mining industry. . . We have lost ground, but we shall regain it in a very short time buy using both our industrial and political machines.[2]

These statements were designed to bolster the miners' flagging spirits, and as Desmarais and Saville claimed, 'without Cook the morale of the ordinary miner would have been much lower, and the erosion of the strength of the MFGB would have been much greater'.[3] In addition, however, Cook was outlining a policy for the future which had two strands. First was the rekindled interest in the formation of a more unified national miners' organisation – a goal of the authors of *The Miners' Next Step*. It is to such aspirations that the National Union of Mineworkers owes its existence. Secondly, for Cook, the defeat of 1926 provoked a sharp shift away from his pure syndicalist reliance on industrial action. His previous disregard for parliamentary activity was replaced by recognition of its importance. From the earliest post-lock-out days Cook expressed his desire to see a Labour government elected as soon as possible.

Arthur Cook's sudden interest in electoral activity resulted from the heavy damage sustained by the MFGB in 1926. For the union defeat entailed decomposition. As Phillips has observed, 'after its final surrender the MFGB was effectively destroyed as a fighting force for almost a decade'.[4] Loss of funds was an obvious result, which precluded any serious thought of industrial action. Secondly, the return to district agreements was more than a symbolic blow to the Federation's unity: gone were the days when the MFGB negotiated for all miners. The disparities and strains which the lock-out had highlighted were now formalised in the bargaining stucture. Furthermore, the MFGB was witnessing the growth of 'non-political' breakaway unionism. Emerging initially in Nottinghamshire under the tutelage of George Spencer, similar (though smaller) developments occurred in other districts. Finally, and perhaps most importantly, the Federation was infected by serious and persistent levels of non-unionism. Unemployment, short-time working, fear of victimisation, low wages, disenchantment and low morale all contributed to falling union membership. The great Miners' Federation, the organisation in which Arthur Cook had placed so much faith, was emasculated.

For Cook the end of 1926 saw a brief respite from the traumas of defeat. The MFGB had been invited to send a delegate to the conference of Russian trade unions, and the Executive nominated Cook to attend. He travelled to the Soviet Union in the first week of December accompanied by Glyn Evans, a CPGB member and ex-miner working for the Labour Research Department. They were given a tremendous reception, a foretaste of the lavish hospitality they received throughout their three-week stay. On the 6th Cook addressed the Russian trades union congress, where he is reported to have claimed that 'a revolutionary situation exists in England'.[5] As British Foreign Office reports noted, Cook told the Russians 'precisely what they wanted of him';[6] and no doubt Cook felt obliged to please the men who had contributed so much to the MFGB's funds during the lock-out.

The Russians soon recognised Cook's exhaustion and ill health, and persuaded him to enter a nursing home for a few days. After three days' rest with good food Cook's energy and vitality returned and he resumed a tour of sightseeing and speeches. According to Evans, Cook was very impressed by the organisation of Russian industry and its trade union movement, considering the Revolution had occurred just nine years earlier. Cook also envied the extent to which Soviet workers appeared to control their industries. At the end of the tour Cook attended the Smolny

Institute in Leningrad, and in Lenin's Room wrote: 'I promise to devote all my powers to Lenin's doctrines and to the colossal work begun by him as his sincere and loving disciple. Long live the Soviets! Long live the Revolution!' He said farewell with the message: 'I return encouraged for the great class war. . . May the English revolution come soon'.[7]

Such remarks, reported at home by a press who assumed Cook was in Moscow to receive rewards from his political masters, merely increased the flow of criticism aimed at the MFGB Secretary's leadership. When the labour leadership – both industrial and political – looked for scapegoats for the debacle of 1926, they turned inward and found a convenient and obvious target. For most within the political and trade union hierarchy, there were two lessons to be drawn from the General Strike. Firstly, it should never happen again. Secondly, there was a shared and clear determination to combat the influence of the Minority Movement and the Communist Party.[8] To such men Arthur Cook epitomised the influences that needed rooting out of the movement. Few can have doubted Cook's sincerity, but most doubted his wisdom. His wild speeches during the lock-out frightened some and astonished others. Furthermore, he was the figurehead of the Minority Movement and close to the Communists. When the labour movement began to debate the causes of the defeat there seemed to be only one on the agenda – A. J. Cook.

In the Parliamentary debate on the coal dispute in December, Ramsay MacDonald accused the government of being baffled by 'Mr Cook's incompetence'. Upon his return from Russia Cook wrote privately to MacDonald asking for an explanation. MacDonald replied contemptuously that 'In all my experience of trade union leadership. . . I have never known one so incompetent as yourself'.[9] In January MacDonald's colleague Philip Snowden wrote a press article in which he claimed Cook had wrecked the MFGB, 'given to the mineowners a power they have never before possessed, given the Conservative government an excuse for lengthening hours and making a general attack upon trade union rights, reduced practically every trade union to a state of bankruptcy and inflicted permanent injury upon British trade'.[10] Further left on the political spectrum, G. D. H. Cole singled Cook out for criticism, and even some sections of the Communist Party were quick to question the quality of Cook's leadership.

Few came to Cook's defence, although he wrote lucid and confident rejoinders to the barrage of accusations which met his return from Moscow: 'Comrades, I do not think I am wrong. Should I have advised the miners to accept longer hours, lower wages and district agreements which, according to my critics, were necessary to carry on the industry and in the miners' own interests?' Did Cook's leadership deserve criticism? It is easy with the benefit of hindsight to accuse him of injurious intractability, and, as Phillips has claimed, 'the miners could almost certainly have escaped some of (the) sacrifices by an earlier readiness to abandon their entrenched bargaining position'.[11] But, as we have seen, Cook's intransigence during the lockout is mythical. It was not easy for him to compromise and yet appear consistent, and it it true that his weekend rhetoric is hard to square with his conference room performances, yet Cook showed a far greater grasp of the dangers facing the miners than did his President. The scope for compromise was, of course, limited. The national officials were tied by conference decisions and district ballots, and one must not underestimate the tremendous fighting spirit of a rank and file which had 'acquired its own ideal of heroic intransigence'.[12] The policy expressed by Cook's slogan 'not a penny off the pay, not a second on the day' was the *result*, not the cause, of the miners' determination. As Cook himself pointed out, 'neither a fool nor a genius can control or dominate the decisions of a million men'. It is, of course, for the reader to form a personal view of Cook's leadership throughout 1926, but the author finds it difficult to accept the traditional criticism that Cook adhered blindly to slogans and shibboleths. Nor is it clear that Cook's weekend oratory should have been a more realistic appraisal of the miners' position. Again with hindsight, perhaps the long-term damage would have been less if Cook had told the miners his innermost thoughts – that they could not win, that compromises and sacrifices were necessary – but as MFGB Secretary he was not prepared to risk damage to the rank and file's resolve. It was comparitively easy for George Spencer to lead men back to work – they were being offered reasonable terms. Arthur Cook knew that such capitulation entailed dire consequences for men in exporting districts. The tragedy for him was that there seemed only two policies that could settle the dispute: surrender or a fight to victory. The former was unthinkable, the second proved impossible. Cook's efforts to promote compromise solutions were spurned by coalowners and government ministers, and he was left with no road to follow. Had he been a harder character emotionally; had he cared less for the men he represented; had he been more selfish and thicker skinned, perhaps he might have told the miners they would be beaten and would have to swallow the consequences. Some might say Cook lacked the courage to be so brutal. The author believes Cook's essential humitarianism was both his key quality and his Achilles heel in 1926.

Throughout 1927 union leaders sought to extinguish troublesome left-wing elements. The Minority Movement had transformed itself, in Dr Martin's words, from 'a comparatively unstructured propaganda campaign into an organised electoral pressure group'.[13] As such the Movement was an anathema to established officials. Early in the year the TUC held an official inquiry into Communist activities within the unions. Walter Citrine wrote a series of articles accusing the CPGB of undemocratic and disruptive tactics. Trades councils were forbidden to affiliate to the Minority Movement, and many individual unions took steps to bar Communists from official positions. For Cook, the only 'key leader of a major union (who) could be counted as a reasonably consistent supporter of the Minority Movement',[14] the situation proved extremely difficult and ultimately untenable.

Concomitant with this attack on extremists was the TUC's clamour for 'industrial peace'. The moderate, conciliatory nature of union leadership became full-blown in the aftermath of the defeat of the General Strike, and early attempts were made to establish a collaborationist relationship with employers. Walter Citrine expressed this policy succinctly: 'the unions should actively participate in a concerted effort to raise industry to its highest efficiency by developing the most scientific methods of production, eliminating waste and harmful restrictions, removing causes of friction and unavoidable conflict'. Scarcely a week went by without some union leader writing enthusiastically about harmony and co-operation with employers. Amidst this sea of moderation Cook alone stood out. As the only Marxist among the union movement's upper echelons, he could often seem isolated. But after 1926 the TUC's dedication to industrial peace threw him into even sharper relief.

The ideological schism within the Labour movement was also present within the MFGB. Political differences within the Federation were, of course, commonplace before 1926, but until that crushing defeat such tensions had usually been submerged in the interests of unity and solidarity. After 1926, however, argument was both frequent and bitter. Arthur Cook, together with Communist and Minority Movement supporters, interpreted the 1926 defeat as proof of the need for the reorganisation of the MFGB into the kind of centralised 'industrial union' first envisaged by the authors of *The Miners' Next Step*. The militants' post-lock-out policy can be summarised as a search for new strength and a challenge to the older, more moderate officials. Increasingly, however, the left within the Federation were confronted by a hostile amalgam of anti-extremists. The moderates included leaders who had joined the left in the struggle to fight off the coalowners before 1926. Herbert Smith, for example, had written in the Communist press in 1925-26 and had supported the CPGB's efforts to gain affiliation to the Labour Party. But after the lock-out Smith became an intolerant and vigorous opponent of Communists and fellow-travellers. This strained the relationship between the MFGB's President and its Secretary. Joseph Jones, a fellow Yorkshireman, defeated by Cook in the Secretaryship ballot in 1924, became an arch-critic of Cook and his allies. As early as October 1926 Jones had announced his intention to 'devote his energies to clearing the coalfields of Communism'. Tom Richards, a survivor of the moderate old guard from within the SWMF, became a major harrier of the militants, as did the other national official, W. P. Richardson of Durham. On the MFGB Executive left-wingers found themselves in a small minority. S. O. Davies, Arthur Horner (who joined the Executive in 1927 but lost his seat the following year) and, from 1928 to 1930, Henry Hicken of Derbyshire, were the only EC members disposed to support Cook. Furthermore, the return to district settlements imposed strains and conflicts. Some district executives were content to work within the November 1926 agreements. The left wing, however, displayed the ambition to recover sufficient bargaining power to overthrow the terms dictated at the end of the lock-out. Cook was the figurehead of the Minority Movement's agitation for a single miners' union, and he also held 'back to the union' meetings in an effort to arrest falling membership.

Cook, then, began to look an isolated figure within the MFGB leadership in 1927. No doubt this caused him discomfort, but what really hurt him were the conditions being suffered by the miners and their families. It became clear during 1927 that the mineowners' recipe for the industry's ills had not worked: lower wages and a longer working day brought no improvement in profitability. Productivity increased, wages costs per ton fell, coal prices fell; but coal was sold at an average loss of 6d per ton. Unemployment ran at twenty-per-cent. Destitution and malnutrition haunted mining valleys and villages. Many miners suffered humiliatingly long periods of unemployment, and thousands were driven to leave their native communities in search of work. Arthur Cook found the conditions in the mining communities heartbreaking. His friend Horner recalled that Cook

> felt personally the tragedy of the men who were out of work and destitute in the coalfields and there used to be a constant succession of callers asking for help at the miners' headquarters in Russell Square.
>
> The unions had no funds to help these people and Cook was giving them money he could not afford out of his own pocket. I used to call in at the office whenever I was in London and used to protest that Cook simply could not afford this charity.[15]

The MFGB, of course, was powerless to promote any fundamental changes that might improve the situation; the Federation's potential was limited to agitation for piecemeal amelioration and alleviation.

Cook's response to the hardships being suffered possessed a characteristic element of direct action. During a speech in the Rhondda he suggested that in order to bring their plight before the government the South Wales miners should 'go to the fountainhead of the trouble' by marching to London. His advice was accepted and in November the march took place. Cook in fact joined the march at Swindon and stayed with it for the remainder of the journey, sharing the rather basic accommodation and the comradeship, occasionally slipping back to Russell Square on official business. On 20 November the march ended with a demonstration in Trafalgar Square, where the rain failed to dampen the enthusiasm of a large audience as it was addressed from the plinth of Nelson's Column by Cook. He told them that 'the great miners' march of 1927 will be remembered as a historic landmark in the struggles of the workers; a warning to Toryism and capitalism. The reverberations of the tramp, tramp, tramp from South Wales to London will live forever.' The march certainly created a form of protest against unemployment that others followed, but its impact on government policy was minimal, and conditions in the coalfields continued to deteriorate.

Cook's participation in the march offered a welcome respite from the tensions of his isolated position as a left-wing leader. On the journey from Swindon to London he renewed acquaintances with old friends and supporters, and Cook seems to have been in fine spirits in their company. Soon, however, he was back to less pleasant business. At the MFGB's annual conference in July Cook had been chosen as one of the Federation's two representatives on the TUC General Council. He was thus installed in a body dominated by Thomas, Bevin, Pugh, Citrine and Ben Turner. Even Tom Richards, the other MFGB member, opposed Cook's militancy. Although Cook's election could be seen as a massive vote of confidence by the miners, the appearance of his isolation within the union movement's leadership was heightened.

Cook's arrival on the TUC GC coincided with an attempt by that body to instigate machinery for joint consultation and negotiation with employers' representatives. In November the GC received an invitation from Sir Alfred Mond (founder of ICI and head of the Amalgamated Anthracite Collieries in South Wales) on behalf of twenty-one other employers, suggesting a meeting with the objects of 'restoration of industrial prosperity and the corresponding improvement in the standard of living of the population'. The General Council allowed some time to elapse before accepting Mond's invitation, and by then Cook had established himself as an exceedingly vocal and troublesome opponent of 'industrial peace'. At his second meeting in October he made a vain attempt to have the GC's minutes made public, and he was often in the press condemning all attempts to reach a *rapprochement* with employers. He questioned the widely held assumption that Britain's economic problems were inevitably temporary and short-term, and his straightforward Marxist analysis was clear:

> Labour leaders who advocate industrial peace do so in many cases because they fondly imagine that the country is on the verge of a trade revival.
>
> I can see no signs of any such revival. We have entered the period of capitalism when permanent trade revival is economically impossible within the present system. . .
>
> Instead of crying for industrial peace we must organize our industrial forces to fight our way out of capitalism.[16]

Cook's whole experience of industrial relations had borne out his belief in the existence of a class struggle. He could not believe that there were benefits to be gained from co-operation with employers; to him the central question remained: 'who has the power?' In the Communist *Sunday Worker* Cook asserted that ' "Industrial peace" under capitalism will be a "peace" dictated by Mond and Londonderry and enforced by a ruthless boss government. Is is to the organized strength of trade unionism we must look if we wish to lead the workers from the chaos and misery of today.'

Cook's opposition to the 'Mond–Turner Talks' (so called because Ben Turner was TUC President) has been dismissed as emotional rather than reasoned.[17] Certainly Cook objected bitterly to the hypocrisy and futility which he believed underlay the discussions. He was disgusted by talk of peace when thousands of miners and their families suffered. He also laid the blame for the MFGB's defeat in 1926 at the door of the same cabal of union leaders which was flirting with the Mond group. However, Cook had reasoned and understandable objections. To him the whole principle of collaboration was contrary to the true function of trade unionism; at a time when capitalism appeared to be entering a period of crisis, he objected to the TUC's efforts to co-operate in its survival. Not surprisingly, given his explicitly Marxist viewpoint, Cook found himself in a tiny minority within the General Council. On 20 December the GC decided by twenty-four votes to three to accept the invitation from the Mond group of employers.

The meetings began in January, and from the outset Cook was an outspoken critic. Opposition to the talks dominated his contributions to the left-wing press. His virulent denunciations and his refusal to be 'bound by any doctrine of collective responsibility'[18] produced several acrimonious exchanges between Cook and other members of the General Council. At one stage Ben Tillett condemned Cook's 'unscrupulous attacks upon his colleagues and his lack of team loyalty' as 'the worst characteristics of a morbid meglomaniac'.

Dissonance had also spread to the MFGB Executive, where Cook and Richards were in conflict over the Mond issue. The Federation leadership's strong stance against militancy had placed Cook in a vulnerable position. He and Horner knew they were fighting a rearguard battle. As early as October 1927 Cook had written to his close friend, warning him: 'you can look out the old school will be after your blood and after mine. Fight we must and fight now'.[19] Cook's most private correspondence was usually scribbled in great haste with little regard for grammar or legibility, and in January 1928 he rushed off another unpunctuated letter to Horner, in which he informed him of his fight against Mondism:

Just a line about the fight what a time I feel like a giant wishing to slay the (cowards?) and traitors. TUC Council afraid to tackle me had nothing but (praise?) from them I went for them attack best form of defence yet failed had 6 others who were turning with me but wanted an excuse only one being no power with Mond & Co. and no mandate from our side. Richards took sides against further meeting until Mond got power from Confederation of Employers and General Council secured mandate (Tom is cute) however we can exploit it. Thomas led the fight but they are in the soup keep up the pressure I am issuing a pamphlet against the mondites. . .

Get South Wales going. Love to all from one in a lone struggle.[20]

Despite these brave words Cook undoubtedly felt ostracised by the moderates who dominated the MFGB Executive and the General Council. At that point his only source of support came from within and on the fringes of the Communist Party. And from even that source Cook was soon to find more problems than comfort.

Cook's relationships with the General Council and his Executive were complicated in the spring of 1928 by joint MFGB-TUC efforts to curb the activities of George Spencer's 'non-political' union in Nottinghamshire. The growth of such right-wing breakaway organisations was a mounting concern to the Federation. Spencer's Nottinghamshire Miners' Industrial Union (NMIU) had by 1928 a larger membership than the official Nottinghamshire Miners' Association. And such breakaways were not confined to that coalfield. The South Wales Miners' Industrial Union had been formed as early as August 1926 and, although small, represented a 'running sore' for the SWMF.[21] By December 1926 similar breakaways had been formed in most coalfields. But it was in Nottinghamshire that the threat to the MFGB was greatest. What were the objectives of the 'non-politicals'? George Spencer apparently held a sincere desire for industrial peace, achieved by a return to the principles of conciliation which dominated industrial relations in the coal industry from the settlement of 1893 to 1910. The corollary of this philosophy was antipathy to militancy in general and to Cook, the Communists and the Minority Movement in particular. In fact, the breakaways, as their titles suggest, were opposed to the linking of miners' unions to any political organisations. Spencer's ideas were suited to what he believed were the best interests of the Nottinghamshire miners, and the relative prosperity of that coalfield ensured his policy of peaceful co-operation was accompanied by reasonable wages. But the non-politicals' philosophy was scarcely suited to the impoverished exporting districts. In circumstances of low wages, mass unemployment and victimisation, with an aggressive ownership seemingly intent on crushing the MFGB, it is difficult to escape the conclusion that 'Spencerism' was not only anachronistic but deceitful and craven. The late Dr J. E. Williams, historian of the Derbyshire miners, had little time for the attempt to establish non-political breakaways: 'The campaign was fundamentally dishonest and was aimed at producing a compliant trade union movement in a time of economic depression. . . The appeals for peace in industry, which formed a prominent part of the "non-political" movement's policy, were appeals for peace at any price.'

Many coalowners appear to have utilised the non-politicals in an effort to increase the emasculation of the MFGB. In areas where the breakaways gained most ground, loyalty to the Federation meant the risk of dismissal. Furthermore, there is some evidence that some employers actully sponsored the non-politicals. Lord Londonderry in the North-East, the Bolsover Colliery Company in Nottinghamshire and Derbshire and the Ocean and Powell-Duffryn companies in South Wales, certainly put some money where their sympathies were.[22] Defenders of the MFGB naturally tended to emphasise the 'company unionism' aspect of the non-politicals, and Cook was no exception. In Derbyshire he asserted that 'without the patronage of the Bolsover Company the organisation could not last a week'. In Nottinghamshire he asked 'whether it could be denied that the Spencer union was a coalowners' union, born in the colliery office. Mr Spencer was only the pawn, the tool and the servant of the coalowners by whom his union was being fostered, encouraged and protected.'

In the spring of 1928 the MFGB enlisted the help of leading trade unionists in an effort to destroy the NMIU. In return, the General Council and the MFGB Executive agreed on 2 March to cease 'personal recriminations both by members and officials of both sides'. Cook was not mentioned by name, but clearly he was the prime target of this pact. The price for the TUC's help in the battle against the non-politicals was the silencing of Arthur Cook. In the second week of March, however, Cook's pamphlet, 'Mond Moonshine' was published. Sub-titled 'My Case Against the "Peace" Surrender', the booklet was a biting critique of the General Council. Cook claimed that 'After the breakdown of the Great General Strike of 1926 – caused by the failure of the leadership of the TUC to pursue courageously the line they had reluctantly adopted – there was a noticeable tendency on the part of these same leaders to take up a conciliatory attitude towards capitalism.' He accused the GC of supporting rationalisation of industry in order to satisfy the employers' desire to re-establish Britain as the 'workshop of the world' – an ambition Cook thought 'futile and hopeless'. The whole pamphlet was a Marxist attack on trade unions' attempts to exist in harmony with employers. Cook saw 'Mondism and non-political unionism as two sides of the same coin: attempts to undermine the true role of working-class political and industrial organisation which was to destroy capitalism and establish socialism. Cook accused the GC of betraying principles, but it was a naïve charge – the TUC leadership had never held the syndicalist ambitions that Cook possessed.

The General Council was incensed by 'Mond Moonshine'. At

its meeting on 28 March, with Cook absent, the GC resolved unanimously to condemn and repudiate the pamphlet, to bring the matter before the MFGB as a breach of the 2 March pact, and to ask the Federation whether it supported its Secretary's actions. Cook's isolation within the Federation leadership was developing rapidly into an open rift. He stated publicly that he was prepared to submit to a ballot of the miners on the question of their confidence in him; Cook stipulated, however, that *all* the MFGB officials should be included in the ballot, 'and then the men could decide whether there should be a change of leadership'. Nevertheless, Cook was not prepared to make the rift into a break which risked his dismissal. When the MFGB Executive discussed the GC's complaints, Cook stated that he had tried to get publication of 'Mond Moonshine' halted in the light of the Nottingham pact. The Executive accepted this explanation, and went on to dissociate itself from the pamphlet and authorised Tom Richards to continue on the GC subcommittee dealing with the Mond group. The General Council was not satisfied and asked for a further meeting with the MFGB. Rumours circulated that Cook was about to be expelled from the GC.

It was at this point that Cook received support from a new direction. It was the left-wing leadership of the ILP who took a stand alongside the MFGB Secretary. The 'Clydsiders' – James Maxton, John Wheatley, David Kirkwood, Campbell Stephen, George Buchanan and, from the CPGB, William Gallacher – shared Cook's opposition to the Mond–Turner talks. A meeting took place between Cook and the Scots at the House of Commons, at which it was decided to issue a manifesto bearing the names of Cook and Maxton. It seems that Cook's role at the stage was purely titular, although the manifesto that was issued in June, addressed to 'the workers of Britain', expressed the humanitarian and sentimental socialism so typical of Cook. The Cook-Maxton manifesto criticised existing trade union and Labour Party leaders for abandoning the principles of the early pioneers of the movement. The left-wingers announced plans for a series of public meetings throughout the country to gauge support for their stance against capitalism: 'Conditions have not changed. Wealth and luxury still flaunt themselves in the face of poverty-stricken workers who produce them. We ask you to join in the fight against the system which makes these conditions possible.'

While Maxton and the Clydesiders naturally channelled their attention to he political wing of the labour movement, Cook pressed ahead with his opposition to the Mond–Turner talks. At a meeting of the General Council at the end of June he joined five others in proposing the ending of talks with the Mond group, although the resolution allowed for discussions with the two formal employers' orgnisation, the Federation of British Industries and the national Confederation of Employers' Organisations. According to *The Times* this meeting also featured an argument between Cook and Thomas which almost resulted in a fist-fight. It is not surprising, therefore, that Cook remained in deep water with his own Executive as well as the GC, and he was under considerable pressure to shut up and conform. He refused to do so. On 4 July the General Council again met the Mond group, and discussed an interim joint report on how the talks had progressed. Cook was the only speaker who objected to the report. His speech, widely quoted in the Communist press, formed the backbone of his new pamphlet, 'Mond's Manacles', which sold 20,000 copies in one month. Cook informed the meeting of businessmen and labour leaders:

> Making capitalism more effective by rationalization will not abolish the workers' subject position in relation to the owners. . . The only rational organization of industry which I recognize is the social organization of industry to serve social ends. The capitalist organi-

zation of industry cannot be rational from the workers' standpoint. The formation of larger productive units, the speeding-up of the workers, the application of science (when profitable) to industry, can only intensify the competitive chaos when the control of industry is in the hands of groups of capitalist whose driving force is (and will always remain) the search for the highest possible profit.

This was a clear, cogent speech. And in the context of Cook's audience, it was a courageous one.

Four days later, on the afternoon of Sunday 8 July, the Cook Maxton campaign was launched at a public meeting in Glasgow. For Maxton the initiative was aimed at releasing the labour movement from the ideological shackles he believed retarded socialism; he informed the ILP's National Administrative Council that the initiative would 'be a sort of Moody and Sankey campaign, conducted rather in the manner of a religious revival'.[23] Cook undoubtedly welcomed the support of the Clydesiders at a time when he was becoming isolated within the MFGB and TUC leadership, although he publicly claimed that 'he and Maxton were out to save the Labour Party'.[24] There is some evidence that Wheatley hoped the campaign would develop into a separate political organisation, but this was a prospect not shared by the other participants. Whatever its aims, however, the campaign depended a great deal on the oratorical performances of Cook and Maxton. The Glasgow meeting, however, fell flat. According to Middlemass, Cook's speech had been written by Wheatley.[25] Scanlon stated that Cook arrived 'with a typewritten dissertation on Marxism which he proceeded to read to the meeting'.[26] The speech, which was reprinted as part of 'Mond's Manacles', was confined to an exposure of the 'errors' of Mondism. It was well-argued, but lacked his customary fire. Worst was to follow: Maxton spoke on the need to work for a Labour government mandated to introduce large socialist measures. His speech was disastrous. Scanlon stated that Maxton was highly strung and 'careful not to say nothing which could be interpreted as an attack on the Labour Party as a party'. Wheatley was furious at Maxton's performance, and withdrew his contribution to the campaign's funds. Cook, however, was apparently quite happy with the way things had gone and left for London in a contented mood.

The campaign continued throughout the summer and autumn, with large meetings in Nottingham, Sheffield and London. According to McNair, the campaign gathered force and 'brought new life to the movement in many towns and districts which had been apathetic and almost despairing'.[27] In fact, the campaign appears to have had little tangible effect. The TUC leadership remained committed to the Mond–Turner talks,and the Mac-Donald–Snowden grip on the Labour Party's policies was un-shaken. Indeed, as the campaign was aimed at the rank and file, it is difficult to see how the initiative could have succeeded where it really mattered – in the places where decisions were taken. Neither Maxton nor Cook were prepared to do anything which would damage the electoral prospects of the Labour Party, and so their whole campaign took on the appearance of a mild agita-tion rather than an attempt to alter Labour policies fundamen-tally. In fact the campaign proved to be divisive within the ILP – the National Administrative Council had only approved of the venture by seven votes to six. For Cook, his now two-pronged attack on 'Mondism' and the moderates condemned his relation-ships with the MFGB Executive and General Council to new heights of acrimony.

In July 1928 the MFGB annual conference met in the North Wales resort of Llandudno. From the outset it was apparent that the ideological struggle within the Federation would dominate proceedings. One of the issues which touched off a bitter right-versus-left battle centred around the activities of the Communist

Party and the Minority Movement in Scotland. In May the MFGB Executive had condemned the Minority Movement and its tactics in attempting to gain official positions within the Scottish miners' union. On the second day of the Llandudno conference an attempt to attend by a Communist delegation from Scotland roused Herbert Smith to leave his chair in order to physically eject the Communists. Arthur Horner, who tried to restrain Smith, was physically assaulted by the MFGB President. On the following day the Executive's criticism of the extremists was endorsed overwhelmingly by the delegates. From that point on the conference witnessed a concerted attack on the left wing – the CPGB, the Minority Movement and non-Communist militants. As the leading left-winger in the Federation, Cook attracted much of the criticism.

When the delegates assembled on the third day of the conference they were able to read a manifesto, published in *The Worker*, bearing the signatures of Cook, Horner, S. O. Davies, Will Lawther, Nat Watkins, William Allan (one of the Scottish Communists who had been targets of Smith's attack), Henry Hicken, Wal Hannington, Tom Mann, Jack Tanner and Alex Gossip. The statement, from the leading militants within the MFGB and some invited celebrity left-wingers, condemned attacks on 'revolutionary trade unionists' and called for an end to the 'policy of co-operation with capitalists to reconstruct capitalism'. The opening debate of the day concerned the Federation's weekly newspaper *The Miner*. In recent months Cook's regular column in the paper had featured his views on the Mond–Turner talks, and he had attacked Tom Richards for supporting the discussions. Joseph Jones of Yorkshire questioned Cook's freedom to write views in *The Miner* which were contrary to MFGB policy. Jones was supported by Herbert Smith, who claimed that 'you cannot write to *The Miner* and to the Communist paper as Cook has been doing'; he did not say why. Only Horner spoke in Cook's defence:

'in my opinion, if you take the personality of Cook out of *The Miner*, *The Miner* is dead. . . It is Cook who sells *The Miner*. There is nothing else in it.' Cook indignantly washed his hands of the paper in the face of the attacks on his contributions: 'so far as I am concerned, I shall not write again to *The Miner*, and therefore, you can have *The Miner* and do as you like with it.'

Cook had a short respite from personal criticism when he was re-elected to the General Council, recording 548 votes to Richards's 307 – an interesting vote of confidence in that a significant number of comparatively moderate delegates supported Cook despite his recent activities. But the conference then debated 'Peace in Industry'. A resolution from the Forest of Dean condemned the Mond–Turner talks. The motion was opposed by Joseph Jones, who devoted his speech to an attack on Cook:

> I deeply regret that Mr Tom Richards should have been traduced in the way he was because of his attendance at that Conference (with the Mond group). He was merely doing openly and above board in meeting employers what Mr Cook saw fit to do in July, 1926. If it was right, expedient or desirable for Mr Cook in July, 1926, to seek a meeting with the employers, with industrialists clandestinely, is it not right for the General Council to do so openly and above board to consider peace in industry now?

Jones's accusations seemed to go unnoticed at this point, and Cook made a long speech defending his attack on 'Mondism'. His remarks also reveal the extent to which he was beginning to feel his position as MFGB Secretary was under threat:

> So far as I am concerned in all this business, my conscience is clear and my hands clean, in spite of the number of lies which have been told. I stand for principles. If you want to take them away, take my job. So far as I am concerned, before you take this job, I will challenge that position, and if you do take it away I shall endeavour

to take a job which will enable me to retain my principles. . .

Cook's speech did not deflect Jones from his attempt to expose Cook's dealings with Rowntree and Layton. Cook denied the charge that he had acted improperly: 'I never attended anywhere with the coalowners or government but what the officials attended with me. I negotiated nowhere with them without the officials. . . I took no steps at any time but that the Committee knew, and after the Committee decided I stood by it, and fought for it.' Jones persisted, however, and Herbert Smith intervened with the promise that an investigation would be held.

The Forest of Dean resolution was defeated by 309 votes to 192, a clear rejection of Cook and the Left's policy, but indicative of the significant minority within the MFGB which supported the militants. Hitherto Cook had been in conflict with his Executive on this issue; but now any further opposition to the Mond–Turner talks would be a flagrant contravention of conference decisions. At the end of the conference an unofficial manifesto was issued by Arthur Horncr and signed by seventeen other prominent MFGB militants, including Cook and Davies. Addressed to all miners' lodges, the manifesto called for a ballot on the question of whether all mineworkers were eligile for membership and elected office 'regardless of their political associations'. The manifesto claimed that a conference composed mainly of full-time officials had taken a decision (to expel the delegation of Scottish Communists) which would break the MFGB and transform it from 'a free and independent Federation of mineworkers into the appendage of a particuar party' (i.e. the Labour Party). A week later Cook asserted that he 'refused to be put down by an Executive which had no solid principles' and he vowed to fight any leader who sought to break, or try to break, the spirit of the militant members of the organization'. Cook was playing a dangerous game. It was unheard of for a MFGB Secretary to be so openly critical of his Executive. He was under great strain and tremendous official pressure, but it is typical of Cook that he reacted in such a defiant manner.

Nevertheless, the tensions of the previous months took their toll. In August Cook suffered a breakdown in his health. On doctor's orders he was forced to take a rest, as he was suffering from 'nerve trouble' and loss of voice. He was back at work within ten days, however – too soon, as events were to show.

In view of his experiences at Llandudno, Cook could have been forgiven for viewing the Trades Union Congress in September with great trepidation. But he continued his campaign against the 'peace talks', and took his policy to the Congress rostrum in a lengthy and emotional speech that was a restatement of his belief in the class struggle and the need for 'one hundred per cent scientific trade unionism that will lead to scientific socialism'. He poured scorn on the Mond group's offer of trade union recognition – 'power will force them to accept recognition' – and he claimed that employers would never surrender their right to victimise. The speech proved such a drain in Cook's energies that he fainted and had to be carried back to his lodgings. The impact of the speech was undermined immediately by Herbert Smith's repudiation of his Secretary's views, pointing out that it was not the MFGB's official policy. Further speeches by J. H. Thomas and Ernest Bevin clinched matters, with the transport workers' leader suggesting that Cook and other critics of the talks were being unrealistic: 'It was all very well for people to talk as if the working class of Great Britain are cracking their shins for a fight and a revolution and we are holding them back. Are they? There are not so many of them as fast as we are ourselves.' The General Council's policy was approved by a massive majority.

Bevin's point is hard to counter: there is little evidence that the TUC's policy was unpopular with rank and file trade unionists.

It is difficult to see what harm existed in the General Council's talks with Mond. No trade union principles were surrendered; and there was the possibility that such contact might dissuade employers from taking full advantage of their powerful position *vis à vis* the unions. Cook himself had adopted much the same sort of attitude as Rhondda miners' agent after the crushing defeat of 1921. Ultimately, however, Cook's scepticism proved justified. When attempts were made to involve the FBI and NCEO in discussions, the employers' organisations rejected the Mond–Turner joint report. Some employers refused to recognise trade unions or forfeit their right to 'dismiss troublemakers'; many employers did not wish to encourage a revival in union membership, and 'many disliked taking action which could restore the prestige of the TUC after the 1926 debacle'.[28] Arthur Cook was not surprised:

> The FBI and NCEO are at least logical in their decisions. They know there can be no peace in industry. . .
> Every leader should know it is power that counts – organized power. . . We can only get what we are strong enough to take, only keep what we have the strength to hold. Let us now drop this hypocrisy, and get on with the real work of organizing a class-conscious working-class army, industrially and politically, to overthrow capitalism and establish socialism.

For Cook the central message of *The Miners' Next Step* was as valid as ever.

Ultimately, the Mond–Turner talks petered out. But in 1928 Cook's policy had been defeated decisively. He found himself in an almost untenable position. He was a lonely figure within the trade union hierarchy; there were opponents within the MFGB and TUC who were after his blood. The investigations into the secret negotiations of July 1926 hung over his head. Horner later confirmed the impression created by Cook's speech at Llandudno, revealing that Cook was seriously considering resignation as MFGB Secretary.[29] It was also apparent to those around him that Cook was a very sick man. Refusing to lighten the massive workload he imposed upon himself, Cook was wrecking his health. Horner recalled tha Citrine and Smith visited Cook in Swansea after his collapse at the TUC rostrum, and warned him he was endangering his life the way he was going on: 'they wanted him to be "sensible", to stop fighting a lone battle'. Cook refused to ease up, and he was to pay a heavy price for his obstinacy and his commitment.

7   Pain and death

The autumn of 1928 was a particularly unhappy time for Arthur Cook. Throughout September and early October he was forced to rest following his collapse at the Trades Union Congress. The minutes of the General Council and the MFGB Executive contain frequent references to Cook's health. Invariably, despite the unpopularity of Cook's politics within these bodies, resolutions were passed expressing sympathy and good wishes. While Cook lay ill the MFGB Executive decided to appoint a three-man sub-committee to inquire into Joseph Jones's allegations regarding Cook's activities in July 1926. The same Executive meeting also discussed Horner's Llandudno manifesto, which two EC members (Davies and Hicken), as well as Cook, had signed. The Executive protested strongly against the manifesto and decided to ask the relevant district associations whether the signatories had received their permission.[1] On resuming his duties Cook was confronted by an Executive angry at his refusal to capitulate to their anti-militant policy. On 12 October the EC again discussed the Llandudno manifesto; replies from the district unions revealed that the signatories had not consulted them before signing. Cook, accountable to the Executive, was apparently threatened with suspension if he did not retract his support for the manifesto. This claim was made by the Communist press, *The Worker* and *Workers' Life*; the MFGB minutes merely record that 'after a long discussion' Cook, Davies and Hicken agreed to withdraw their signatures from the manifesto, pending the findings of an inquiry into the position in Scotland. Historians have concluded that this was a climb-down in the face of official pressure.[2] Hicken, however, denied this, and Cook seems to have been happy with the outcome. But perhaps he was trying to put on a brave face in circumstances where he had suffered a defeat at the hands of his Executive:

> Everything is now practically cleared up so far as I am concerned, and there is nothing hanging over my head. The investigations of Mr Jones's allegations is not quite completed, but the Executive know what was behind my action and when I print all the fact it will be seen that I was working in the interests of the miners. The TUC General Council's complaint has also been cleared out of the way. I took the line today that I could no longer go on if this hostile attitude were maintained. Things are now all right. On the Scottish position there is to be a Scottish inquiry by the Federation, and that is what I have all along demanded.[3]

Things were far from all right for Arthur Cook, however. His retraction of the Llandudno manifesto opened the floodgates for torrents of criticism from the Communist Party, the source of so much support for Cook since his rise to national prominence. For several months the CPGB had been adopting a new, more extreme attitude. Stalin's call for an aggressive departure from the policy of supporting the Labour party was attractive to an influential minority within the CPGB who had become disenchanted by the lack of progress of this line and the recent attacks on Communists mounted by the labour movement's leadership. This element within the CPGB began to argue for a policy which entailed an attack upon all those who failed to support revolutionary policies. Stalin himself served notice of the 'new line' when he described George Lansbury, Maxton and Fenner Brockway – all on the far left of the Labour Party – as 'worse than enemies'.[4] The minority within the CP who supported this view – led by R. Palme Dutt and Harry Pollitt – felt the Party should form an 'alternative leadership in total opposition to the Labour Party'.[5]

Gradually this view dominated the CPGB; all Labour candidates, from MacDonald and Thomas to Maxton and Wheatley, received unrestrained vilification from the CP's columnists. Cook's record and his continued support for Communists had exempted him from attack, but this all ended in October 1928. The *Sunday Worker*'s headlines announced: 'COOK COMPROMISES', and Arthur Horner was in print to condemn the action of Cook, Davies and Hicken as 'a very serious concession' which 'they will live to regret': 'if Cook can only retain his job by participation in the treachery of his enemies, it would have been better to let them carry on with the threat (of suspension) and so bring the issues right to the doorstep of the members.'[6]

Cook replied to such criticism by announcing his intention to oppose any 'outside elements' who sought the 'object of wrecking or weakening of the miners' organization. This was an obvious reference to the CPGB and Minority Movement. This apparent volte-face in Cook's attitude could be interpreted as a sell-out of his left-wing allies, perhaps under the manipulation of the MFGB Executive. The truth, however, is that the full repercussions of the CPGB's ultra-left policy were beginning to emerge and dawn on Arthur Cook. Perhaps the most controversial aspect of the Communist 'new line' was its opposition to existing unions and its efforts to build new, revolutionary, organisations. Cook would have no truck with this. He was Secretary of the MFGB and held immutable views about the sancitity of solidarity and unity: his long-held ambition had been to see a centralised national union, not more breakaways. In Scotland the right-wing leadership had used every constitutional device and loophole to frustrate the CPGB and Minority Movement's democratically achieved advances. But at the end of 1928 it was the Communists who appeared disruptive and destructive as they began to consider the formation of an alternative union. In April 1929 the CPGB set up the United Mineworkers of Scotland. The Communists no doubt felt that the maneouvrings of the right-wing in the official union had left them little alternative, but on this issue Cook broke with them, and they broke with him.

In March 1928 Cook had declared that 'stoppages in the present circumstances of the coal trade would be utterly ineffective in improving the position of the men'. By the end of that year Cook was becoming increasingly preoccupied by the hardship caused by unemployment: 'the great mining community amounts to about five milion souls, almost one-eighth of the whole population of this country. It is suffering from one of the worst kinds of plague ever experienced in the history of civilization, the plague of poverty, unemployment, underemployment'.[7] Writing in the ILP's *New Leader*, Cook complained of the 'Massacre of the Miners', and called for a programme of public works, early retirement at sixty for miners, and the raising of the school-leaving age. He also suggested the suspension of the Eight Hours Act. At the end of October he consented to write his 'Secretary's Review' once again in *The Miner*. Here too unemployment was the issue that overrode other matters:

> I have yielded to the numerous requests from readers and branches to return to the pages of our paper, realizing that whilst an official has rights he has responsibilities; while he has dignity he has duties. The terrible conditions of our coalfields, with unemployment and poverty growing worse every day, must be the first claim upon any leader's services. There should be no division in regard to the necessity for immediate steps to save the mining community from starvation. To that task, with others, I have set my hand.

In that article Cook signposted the nature of his leadership under the conditions which afflicted the coal industry. Nineteen twenty-nine brought little relief. A slight improvement in demand for coal occurred: unemployment in the coalfields fell from the 1928 high of twenty-eight per cent but still averaged sixteen per cent in 1928. Cook's articles in *The Miner* displayed increasing concern with the distress of mining communities. Such was his anxiety, Cook overlooked his dispute with the CPGB in order to help them organise another march to London. In so doing he opposed Herbert Smith and W. P. Richardson, who had condemned the march as futile. In March Cook appeared at the Marlborough Street Police Court to plead on behalf of three Rhondda miners who had been arrested for singing for money.

In that month the MFGB sent a delegation to meet Baldwin to express the Federation's concern at the hardship suffered by its members. Cook urged the government to introduce reorganisation, but Baldwin was not prepared to impose reforms on the industry. Four days later Cook made it clear that he looked to a Labour victory at the next election as the miners' only hope of improvement: 'It is the bounden duty of all of us to put on one side disagreements or personal differences and work for a majority Labour government.'[8]

The CPGB was appalled by Cook's alignment with Labour. As early as January Palme Dutt, the CP's leading theoretician of the 'new line', had denounced the possibility of achieving a 'socialistic transformation' of the Labour Party, and had condemned the Cook–Maxton campaign as 'in practice nothing better than organised hypocrisy'. To the CPGB, Cook's support for Labour implied a complete collapse of principles. Cook's complete break with the CPGB came with the establishment of the breakaway United Mineworkers of Scotland. Cook was horrified: 'I warn all mineworkers in Britain and in Scotland against this move of the Communist Party, which cannot succeed because the workers of Britain will not allow it.' As Dewar has observed, for Cook 'the formation of the union was the final confirmation of his belief that the party was no longer in the workers' camp'.[9] On 12 April he and Richardson reported to the MFGB Executive on the Scottish situation. Cook in the past had protested against the tactics of the right-wing officials in the coalfield, but he, Smith and Richardson signed a denunciation of the creation of new unions and of 'the continued interference of the Communist Party (Minority Movement) and other bodies in the business of the MFGB and its affiliated organizations'.

In the eyes of the CPGB Cook's treachery was now complete. Cook no doubt expected the Party's ire to cascade upon him, but it is most unlikely that he had prepared himself to be publicly condemned by his closest friend Arthur Horner. Horner himself had grave reservations about the CP's new union tactic, but he launched himself into a scathing criticism of Cook's support for the Labour Party. His open letter to Cook was printed in the *Workers' Life*:

> Dear Arthur,
>   So you have joined the enemies of the revolutionary struggle in Britain! . . .
>   I am not happy to find that Cook is like the rest. . . You call for a Labour government as the workers' salvation when you know – how well you know! – that this is cheating the workers. . . The Labour Party is a capitalist party, and the Labour government will be a capitalist government. They are and will be anti-working class, and he who supports either is an enemy of the workers, regardless of the label he wears or the hidden motives he seeks to realize.

Cook's typewritten reply, sent privately to Horner on 15 April and printed in the *Workers' Life* on the 26th, is a lucid exposition of Cook's policies and tactics under conditions of mass unemployment, hardship and the industrial impotency of the MFGB:

> Dear Arthur,
>   You have neither done yourself justice nor been fair to me in your letter published in 'Workers' Life'. Owing to our long and closely connected comradeship, I am constrained to reply, hoping

yet that we can reconcile our differences and still continue our comradeship which was forged in the class struggle.

You know that you are wrong when you state I have joined the enemies of the revolutionary struggle – neither have what you term the Trade Union and Labour Party bureaucracy got hold of me – nor have I given up the struggle for a National Mine Workers' Union which will include all mine workers and an all-including world wide International of Mine Workers including our Russian Mine Workers. I am as strong today as ever in my desire and determination to secure these objects. I have and shall continue to oppose 'Mondism' because I am working and fighting for Socialism. You know as well as I the terrible conditions in the coalfields and the suffering of our women and children. I have been compelled to do the most unpleasant task of begging for food, money, boots and cast-off clothing. Practically every day young men stranded, call for food, clothing and shelter at my office (you have seen them). I have done my best for them. Every day the post brings letters to me and Mrs Cook begging for help, especially from expectant mothers, terrible epistles of agony and despair. Even from Mardy, where men and women have fought heriocally against great odds.

Following this emotional appeal for understanding of the conditions pertaining to his policies, Cook proceeded to outline the measures he believed were necessary to provide some relief:

What are the means of changing these conditions, which I know you must want changed as well as I? An immediate application of the policy I know you agree with – repeal of the Eight Hours Act, Minimum Wage Act, Pensions at Sixty, raising school age and the age of entering the pits, adequate compensation, nationalization of mines, minerals and by-products.

This policy contained planks which the MFGB had successfully argued for inclusion in the Labour Party's election manifesto. Cook went on to criticise the CPGB's tactics of forming new unions and opposing the Labour Party:

To accomplish this we need industrial and political organization, in short, power. We can only get what we are strong enough to take, only keep what we have the strength to hold. That being so, you must agree that to secure power we must strengthen and reorganize our industrial and political movement. The trade union and the Labour Party is the medium whereby the masses find expression – 'the workers' army'.

This cannot be done by forming new unions, thus dividing the workers and intensifying the struggle between workers and leaders in our present weakened state. Such a course would enable the owners to strengthen their power and increase persecution and victimization of the active comrades at the pits. You know well that we have too many trade unions now in operation, hence the only way is for members to take a hand reorganizing and centralizing their unions. I believe the members desire this, and it can be achieved if they would attend their branch meetings and propose this change. It would take time, but if the members so desire it can be accomplished.

The policy of working inside the unions for change is the only way to secure them. In regard to the tactics of the Communist Party in opposing Labour candidates, I have always opposed this and I feel sure you cannot agree it is the right thing to do. It divides the workers and gives power to our enemies. Knowing you believe in the programme outlined above, I cannot understand your desire to oppose the party that is pledged to it. As you know, the next election means putting the Tory Party or the Labour Party in power. I cannot believe that you want to return the Tory Party, after the experience we have just gone through.

In his autobiography, Horner wrote: 'Arthur Cook and I were like brothers and when we quarrelled we quarrelled like brothers and our quarrels were very bitter indeed, but we remained friends and comrades to the end. There was very little I disagreed with in Arthur Cook's letter, but this question of whether we should challenge the Labour Party or not was one where I felt, in the circumstances at that time, we had to show our opposition to the prevailing right-wing policies.' For Cook however, 'shows of opposition' were a luxury when miners and their families were starving. He could not afford to sit on the sidelines and become embroiled in doctrinal debates. The Labour Party provided the means for immediate improvements, and Cook was not prepared to spurn that opportunity, no matter how disagreeable he found most of the party's leadership. Cook dismissed the CPGB's grandiose programme for a 'revolutionary workers' government' as 'platitudes'.

From April onwards the *Workers' Life* maintained weekly attacks on Cook. Very little good was said of Cook by *any* political group at this time, in fact. Only his old ally S. O. Davies voiced public praise, noting that Cook had attracted the calumny of all shades of political opinion:

> he has brought crashing to the ground, inextricably mixed beyond all hope of identification, ideologies, bourgeois and revolutionary. . . for several years past I have worked in the closest, most intimate contact with A. J. Cook. I still regard him, temperamentally and ideologically, as a splendid product of working class life.
>
> During our active acquaintance he and I have noted the passing of many of his traducers from our Movement to the limbo of bourgeoisdom. But A. J. Cook still stands the most complete embodiment of that revolutionary spirit that will untimately free the workers from the thrall of capitalism.

These were brave words of friendship that must have given Arthur Cook great comfort.

Cook's enthusiasm for a Labour government was magnified by MacDonald's pre-election promises of action to deal with the coal industry. On 26 March Smith, Cook, Richards and Richardson met MacDonald, Thomas, Lansbury, Snowden and

Tom Shaw to discuss the inclusion of proposals for the industry in Labour's election manifesto. MacDonald informed the MFGB officials that nationalisation would not be possible in the first session of parliament, but that a Labour government would 'proceed with the immediate problems confronting the industry and affecting the welfare of the men'. The specifics of this policy were: repeal of the Eight Hours Act, raising school-leaving age, retirement at sixty, and the suspension of recruitment from outside the industry. MacDonald also promised that 'the larger programme of nationalization of mines, minerals and by-products would be proceeded with after the first essentials had been dealt with'. Cook was delighted with these pledges, which he claimed were 'sealed and signed' in his desk.

Such was his anxiety to see a Labour government, Cook even consented to speak in support of MacDonald, who was a candidate in the Durham mining constituency of Seaham Harbour. This completed the rift between Cook and one of his old allies Harry Pollitt, who was standing against MacDonald for the Communist Party. In the general election all but four of the Communist candidates (including Pollitt) lost their deposits; in the coalfields all forty-three MFGB-sponsored Labour candidates were elected. In total, Labour won 287 seats, the Conservatives 261 and the Liberals 59. Arthur Cook was thrilled, and expressed the hope that the government would implement the 'Miners Charter' of pre-election pledges. In the aftermath of Labour's victory Cook seems to have formalised his alienation from the CPGB and his alliance with Labour: on 12 June *The Times* reported that he had rejoined the ILP as a member of the London Central branch. In view of recent events this move was not entirely surprising. What was unusual, however, was the high degree of public tolerance Cook displayed towards the government in its efforts to honour its manifesto commitments to the MFGB.

The miners were understandably anxious that MacDonald

should introduce the promised legislation, and Cook make public reference to his belief that 'the workers' faith in political action was in the hands of the government'. At the same time, however, Cook recognised that the coal industry's dire economic position and the government's minority standing raised many difficulties. He accepted MacDonald's promise of legislation in the autumn session of parliament, and at the MFGB's annual conference in July his cautious line attracted criticism from militants who demanded a more positive approach which cared less for the government's survival. Cook and his Executive's reluctance to push MacDonald too hard was intensified by their realisation that the coalowners would demand wage cuts in compensation for reduced hours should the Eight Hours Act be repealed. This was a consideration which militants seemed prepared to ignore. As it transpired, however, the belligerence of the Mining Association, added to the government's weak position and the MFGB's industrial impotence, were to put severe strain on any spirit of partnership and tolerance which existed between the Cabinet and the MFGB leadership. The poor economic position of the coal industry created fundamental problems: the government were aware that reductions in hours without wage cuts would force many collieries to close, adding to unemployment figures that were already severe. The Cabinet was also aware that drastic reorganisation, involving rationalisation, nationalisation of mining royalties, and cartelisation of selling coal, was essential to finance losses in the export sector by creating large profits inland.

On 23 July the government announced plans for the introduction of district sales cartels. The Mining Association, meanwhile, gave early notice of its recalcitrance by refusing to discuss with the MFGB possible consequences of a reduction of hours. By autumn the government had formed a Cabinet Coal Committee to draft legislation and negotiate with the miners and coal owners. Soon Cook was urging the government to stick to its pre-election position and complained that ministers were too easily influenced by coalowners. On 16 October the Cabinet Coal Committee made a compromise proposal of a seven-and-a-half hour day. Herbert Smith, whose Yorkshire miners were already working a seven-and-a-half hour day, accused the government of cowardice. Cook complained that the March pledges had been broken, either through 'ignorance or with the intention of getting votes without intending to supplement it by acting'.[10] The Federation leadership faced a difficult dilemma: they had a duty to those miners for whom a seven-and-a-half our day was no advance, but they were also aware that obduracy might wreck the government and lose the potential for future progress. At a MFGB special conference at the beginning of November, delegates agreed reluctantly to accept the government proposal. The Yorkshire delegates walked out in disgust, and were joined by Herbert Smith who resigned the Federation Presidency.

Writing in *The Miner*, Cook defended the government's offer and the MFGB's decision to accept it. He expressed his fear that even a seven-and-a-half hour day would prompt demands for wage reductions from the Mining Association, and he was most anxious that the government stand by the MFGB and introduce reorganisation in order that wage levels be maintained when the shorter day came into effect. He told an Accrington audience: 'We have been loyal to the government, and I have risked my career in giving them my wholehearted support, but if they fail us our faith and trust will be broken in political action.'

The government's Coal Mines Bill was introduced to the House of Commons early in December. In addition to the seven-and-a-half hour day, the Bill proposed subsidisation of exports by national and district levies, and the limitation of output through production quotas. There was no mention of a safeguard for miners' wages, and nothing to improve efficiency. The aim of the Bill was to raise coal prices by artificial restriction of output. However, the MFGB's appetite for labour-saving rationalisation had diminished in the face of mass unemployment, and Cook was pleased with the Bill, believing it was 'a real contribution to the solution of some of the problems of the industry... a first great step to national control'. On 19 December the Bill passed its second reading by just eight votes, with forty-four Liberals voting against it.

The miners' leaders had very little choice but to support the Bill. With little over half the workforce in the MFGB, the Federation was powerless. Cook believed that it was only the existence of a Labour government that had dissuaded the owners from demanding wage cuts on the eight-hour day. His support of the government undermined his reputation as a militant, but his policy was based on common sense. He recognised the limitations to the opportunities presented by a minority administration: 'such a Labour government can only be somewhat of an ambulance brigade doing rescue and relief work'.[11] And he was aware of the dangers ahead:

> We may have to face some time in 1930 an industrial struggle, as the coalowners have threatened a reduction in wages if hours are reduced, and that the miners will not stand whatever the consequences. There may also be a general election. A minority government on sufferance is neither pleasant nor productive. For these possible events we must make full preparation.

The early months of 1930 proved a frustrating time for the miners. The Mining Association maintained its traditional opposition to measures designed to limit output and control prices. Collieries closed, but the owners were opposed to any systematic programme of closure or amalgamation. Their industrial philosophy, as in 1926, was totally unsuited to conditions of falling demand. The Mining Association set out to destroy the

Coal Bill, using Conservative MPs to delay and obstruct in the Commons, reinforced by a bloc of titled coalowners in the Lords. The Mining Association formulated a scheme which allowed a 'spread-over' of hours, whereby ninety hours per fortnight could be worked instead of seven-and-a-half hours a day. With short-time working prevalent, the 'spread-over' was intended to allow the perpetuation of an eight-hour day in the exporting districts. This attack on the Bill stung Cook into some aggressive talk:

> The miners are not yet broken, and if we are forced to fight we will fight for victory. . . I issue a call to our people. While desirous for peace, let us prepare for war by organizing on a 100% basis. . . I have done my best to secure a peaceful settlement in the mining industry, but our claims have been largely ignored, and our patience has been abused. I, therefore, take my stand in urging the miners, in the event of this Bill being defeated, to take national action to improve their conditions.

The Bill struggled through the Commons reasonably unscathed. But in the Lords an amendment allowing the 'spread-over' was moved successfully by Lord Gainford, vice-president of the Mining Association. The owners calculated that the government would accept the amendment rather than lose the entire Bill, and that MacDonald would not risk an election on the issue. The owners were correct. On 15 July the Cabinet told the MFGB Executive of its dilemma, and by ten votes to nine the miners agreed to the 'spread-over' on condition the scheme could not be operated without the consent of the relevant district associations. Cook stated that his Executive were 'torn between patience and revolt', without revealing which way he had voted. The Coal Mines Bill became law on 1 August, and Cook declared that he and the Executive would work to make it a success.

During this period Cook's leadership was characterised by pragmatism and little militancy. At MFGB conferences he appeared to be a disarmer of over-ambitious talk, much as he had been during the 1926 lock-out. He frequently employed his long-standing slogan that 'it is only power that counts'; and no matter how much Cook desired to restore miners' conditions to pre-1926 standards, he was prepared to admit that such progress was not possible in the short term.

As it transpired, for coalowners in exporting districts even a half-hour reduction in hours was unpalatable. Invariably there were demands for wage cuts unless the 'spread-over' was operated. The main trouble-spot, unsurprisingly in view of economic conditions and the attitude of coalowners, was South Wales. At the end of September Cook warned of impending battle, and at the end of November the South Wales coalowners announced general wage reductions. Facing a lock-out if they did not submit either to the 'spread-over' or the wage cuts, the SWMF applied to the MFGB for permission to implement the 'spread-over'. On 28 November a MFGB special conference considered the SWMF's request, and Cook make it clear he favoured a further compromise on hours in order to avoid either a stoppage or lower wages: 'It is a time to be courageous and honest enough to face the facts of the whole situation. . . Take South Wales with those men involved, and the number organized, will it not cause disintegration? Whatever we may say a struggle cannot be faced. . . with the ammunition we have got to fight with what hope is there of success?' The delegates, however, refused permission for the 'spread-over'. Cook was alarmed: 'In the light of that decision I am all anxiety for the future of the Federation.'

Fortunately, a compromise settlement was negotiated in South Wales, with the 'spread-over' operating for one month while negotiations continued. Ramsay MacDonald urged the MFGB to agree to a three-month trial of the 'spread-over', and at a MFGB special conference on 4 December Cook advised delegates to accept this proposal. In his efforts to dissuade delegates from pursuing a course likely to result in industrial struggle, Cook painted a very rosy picture of future possibilities in the coal industry. He regarded the Coal Mines Act as evidence that the miners' fortunes would prosper under a Labour government, albeit slowly. The reality, of course, included a very bleak immediate future. Nevertheless Cook's optimistic portrayal is understandable, coming as it did from a man still haunted by the spectre of 1926. In 1930, with the miners in a vastly inferior strategic position, Cook feared that industrial action would impose irresistible strains on the MFGB. To those delegates who pushed for an aggressive policy, Cook gave a curt warning: 'We have played the Communists' game. They want to destroy. They have sent out circulars. It is another revolution, but it means destruction to our own people.'

The MFGB conference accepted Cook's advice and withdrew from contemplation of national industrial action. In South Wales, however, the situation turned sour. The coalowners, flushed with power and bitterly opposed to any reduction in hours, offered only a one-month trial period on the basis of a ninety-hour fortnight. Negotiations failed and on New Year's Day 1931 the South Wales miners were on strike.

The Coal Bill and its subsequent problems dominated MFGB business throughout 1930. But the problems which caused Cook and the MFGB so much distress were not confined to the coal industry. In January 1929 there had been 1.4 million unemployed; by March 1930 the figure had reached 1.75 and was still rising. The Labour administration was at a loss to deal with the problem. MacDonald confessed to his diary that he was baffled. Philip Snowden at the Exchequer stuck rigidly to the Treasury view that the world depression would eventually correct itself and that in the meantime it was the government's task to balance the books and keep public spending in line with national income.

What Skidelsky has termed the administration's 'intellectual bank-ruptcy'[12] was reflected in the choice of J. H. Thomas as minister with special responsibility for employment. The only figure within the government who seemed capable of escaping the rigid economic orthodoxy insisted upon by Snowden was Oswald Mosley, a young crusading politician who appeared most uncom-fortable as one of Thomas's junior ministers. In January 1930 Mosley presented a memorandum on the unemployment question to MacDonald. It contained proposals for a large-scale public works programme, state control of banking and credit policy, and a long-term programme of economic reconstruction based on government planning. The Mosley memorandum was in direct conflict with Snowden's conservative beliefs, and MacDonald remained loyal to his longstanding right-hand man. On 19 May Mosley's memorandum was rejected by the Cabinet; the following day he resigned.

Following his departure Mosley attempted to mobilise Labour Party and trade union support for his policy. Arthur Cook needed little encouragement to support a more active approach to the unemployment problem, and came out publicly in favour of Mos-ley. Cook's friendship with Mosley dated back to the 1926 lock-out, when the young politician had campaigned on the miners' behalf. For this he had never been forgotten by the MFGB, who regularly supported Mosley's candidature for the Labour Party's National Executive committee. Cook and Mosley also had a mutual friend in John Strachey, who had edited *The Miner*. The MFGB, however, in the policy struggle between Mosley and the Labour Party leadership, backed MacDonald and Snowden. At the Labour Party annual conference in October the MFGB's massive block vote was cast against a resolution calling for Mosley's proposals to be debated. On this issue Cook was, once again, out of step with his Executive. At a meeing of the TUC General Council later that month Cook proposed that the Council should 'give an opportunity to Sir Oswald Mosley to prove whether his proposals on unemployment were practical'; but Tom Richards prompted the decision to take no action.[13]

By December 1930 over two million people were out of work, and Mosley pushed ahead with his campaign. His memorandum was given a stronger left-wing hue by Strachey, Nye Bevan and another Labour MP, W. J. Brown, and published as the Mosley Manifesto. The document called for protection of the home market, public works, increased social services spending, long-term rationalisation of the economy, and a more dynamic and efficient Cabinet structure to implement this policy. The Mosley Manifesto was signed by seventeeen Labour MPs and one other – Arthur Cook. The manifesto had little impact on government policy, however, and Mosley began to consider the need to form a new political party. The extent to which Cook would have participated in this enterprise is clouded by his illness and long periods in hospital during 1931. When Mosley's New Party was formed early that year its eventual fascist nature was not immediately apparent. In April the New Party stood against Labour in a by-election at Ashton-under-Lyne. Mosley certainly was visiting Cook in hospital at this time, and apparently Cook expressed support for the New Party but refused to back it publicly 'until the Miners' Federation had definitely broken with Labour'.[14] In July, however, Strachey broke with Mosley, anxious at the way the New Party was developing, and Cook's involvement seems to have ended at this point also. Soon afterwards Cook was back in hospital fighting for his life.

The last months of Arthur Cook's life were dominated, of course, by pain and illness. For some contemporaries and historians Cook's deteriorating physical condition after 1926 explains his break with the extreme left wing and his support for policies which were moderate in comparison with his past record. It seems certain that Cook was a very sick man throughout this period. It is doubtful whether he ever recovered from the awesome strain he experienced throughout 1926. Fatigue, nervous exhaustion and hoarseness appear to have been constant burdens on Cook. His most serious ailment, however – and the one which probably killed him – was his leg. Since 1926 he had obstinately refused to have proper treatment, and the wound deteriorated. And yet, before 1931, this does not seem to have prevented Cook from travelling and addressing meetings. Contemporaries such as Fenner Brockway and Robin Page Arnot have attributed Cook's moderation to their belief that Cook's illness reduced his contact with the rank and file and undermined his capacity to express radical ideas in rousing speeches. It is my belief, however, that Cook's leadership between 1928 and 1930 was consistent with a genuine recognition of the MFGB's weakness and the dire need for alleviation of the suffering in the coalfields. His break with the Communists was caused by fundamental differences over policy, not by any mental or moral collapse on Cook's part. His support for MacDonald's government was pragmatic and by no means uncritical – not a 'sell-out' of principles. Cook said 'it is power that counts' so often that perhaps it has been overlooked; the fact is that Cook's leadership was based on that fundamental belief. In the last two or three months of his life, when Cook knew he was dying, the spirit seems to have left him, but until then Cook's views were consistent and logical.

Nineteen thirty-one opened with a strike in the South Wales coalfield and Cook already seriously ill. His leg injury was causing insufferable pain, and he agreed at last to enter hospital for treatment. He was admitted to the Manor House Hospital in Golders Green on 9 January. He had made strenuous efforts to avert the South Wales stoppage, but at this point Cook attempted to elicit government support for the strikers. On the day he entered hospital Cook wrote the following private letter to Ramsay MacDonald:

> Dear Mr Prime Minister,
>
> I think you should know how some of us feel in regard to the action of the Labour Cabinet towards the mineworkers. I am terribly disappointed at the shabby way our men have been treated in the face of the attacks of the coal owners especially in South Wales. I think a Labour government would defend its own Mines Act and put up a fight against the coal owners attacking the mineworkers – but no – we are left to battle alone against the most vicious set of capitalists existing in this country. We have had nothing but lavish promises from a Labour government which makes it difficult and impossible for some of us to defend (it) in the future. It appears to me that our only hope is in our trade union movement. Had it not been for the splendid fight put up by the South Wales miners, huge reductions would have been forced upon them.
>
> Yours faithfully,
> A. J. Cook[15]

These words are defiant, and evidence that Cook had not lost his capacity for angry criticism of MacDonald. In view of the SWMF's and MFGB's position they were also desperate words. Cook's exasperation failed to move the prime minister. While MacDonald's reply was not as contemptuous as his letter to Cook in January 1927, he gave the MFGB Secretary's complaints short shrift:

> My dear Cook,
>
> I have your letter of the 9th January, but for the moment I am concerned with your own health. I do hope that your sojourn in hospital will completely restore you.
>
> When you are out and about again I will reply to your letter, and I can assure you there will be a few brickbats in it, as I am getting sick and tired of the way that some of you get your men into difficulties and then turn to the government and say, 'If you

do not get us out, we will tell how disgusted we are with you.'
Yours very sincerely,
JRM [16]

On 15 January the MFGB Exexutive received a letter informing them of Cook's illness; Tom Richards, President of the Federation following Herbert Smith's resignation, stated that Cook 'had been carrying on under great difficulties for several months, and had shown great fortitude in discharging those duties when suffering from severe pain and lameness'. The Executive discussed the South Wales strike, and contemplated sympathetic action. Such was the MFGB's industrial weakness, however, the EC merely invited districts to make financial contributions to the SWMF. In circumstances of low union membership the South Wales miners put up a brave fight, but they could not endure a protracted struggle. On 16 January the SWMF negotiated a settlement on the basis of a two-month interval during which wages would not be reduced and the dispute would go to arbitration. The arbitration board, under the chairmanship of F. P. M. Schiller, advised wage reductions dependent on family responsibilities – a means-tested wage cut. Spasmodic unofficial strikes broke out in protest, but reluctantly the SWMF decided to abide by the arbitration.

On 19 January Arthur Cook's right leg was amputated just above the knee. In a note from his secretary (obviously written before the operation but dated 31 January in the MacDonald Papers), the prime minister was informed: 'Mr Citrine's secretary tells me that Mr Cook has got to have his leg amputated, he has no choice in the matter if he wishes to live. The Manor House Hospital said that he was a very sick man, and it may be months before he is able to come out.'[17] Cook was reported to have withstood the operation well, although he was agitated by worry that the disability would force him to surrender his job. At a

179

MFGB Executive meeting on 28 January it was reported that Cook 'was recovering well from the operation and was most cheerful in the circumstances'.

Within six weeks of his operation Cook was back at work equipped with a cork leg and crutches. In order to carry out his duties Cook purchased a car, and the MFGB Executive resolved to pay for the car and grant Cook £75 for one year in order that he could employ a chauffeur. The Executive also told Cook he should take a lengthy holiday in order to recuperate fully.

Cook took no holiday, however, and plunged back into his work. On 19 March a vital MFGB conference met to debate the current hours and wages position, in the knowledge that in July Baldwin's Eight Hours Act would expire and a seven-hour day would return automatically. All delegates realised that under such circumstances the Mining Association would demand widespread and heavy wage reductions. The Coal Mines Act had failed to improve the industry's economic performance. Any hope that shorter hours and output restriction would produce higher prices and wages had proved illusory under circumstances of fierce international competition and worldwide depression. Cook told the conference that under prevailing conditions 'wages cannot be increased by a reduction in hours... Our hopes of three months have been in vain.' He believed that the operation of the 'spread-over' of hours until June would safeguard wages. Then the expiration of the Eight Hours Act would give the miners greater bargaining power on the wages issue. The conference preferred a more ambitious alternative strategy, however: the MFGB would seek to amend the 1912 Minimum Wage Act to protect wages.

Cook was unable to play his customary part in the MFGB's campaign. It is obvious that he had not recovered from his operation. In March he belatedly took the holiday that no doubt he should have taken immediately after his discharge from hospital.

He returned to work in April, but was incapacitated again towards the end of that month. He watched as the MFGB pressed the government for a £2 10s minimum wage. The government, however, seemed unwilling to or incapable of coercing the Mining Association to abandon its intransigent position. In June Cook revived an old battle slogan when he delcared that 'peace with poverty is no longer possible in the British coalfields'. But he was too ill to mount a campaign in support of the MFGB's claim. No doubt he was also aware that under existing economic conditions the MFGB's demands were not feasible without massive colliery closures in the exporting districts.

At the end of June a MFGB conference met to appraise developments. It had become clear that the government were not going to deliver the MFGB's demands, while the Mining Association was intent on demanding wage reductions in every district when the working day reverted to seven hours. Confronted by hard facts, the Executive were prepared to compromise and accept a seven-and-a-half-hour day for one year, on existing wage rates which would become the legal minimum wage in future. Cook believed the miners could not expect anything better. Some militants, notably Noah Ablett, urged the MFGB to demand a minimum wage bill regardless of the danger to the government's survival. Cook clashed with his old ally, claiming that such a policy would risk the return of the Tories and massive cuts in the workforce. Cook's speech lacked Ablett's passion but also his impracticality. At a further conference on 2 July Cook again recommended a cautious policy of acceptance of a government offer of a seven-and-a-half-hour day on existing wage rates:

> It is no use wanting what we cannot get. . . The alternative of these proposals means that we must fight. If you decide to fight, then this Federation will be smashed to smithereens. . .

181

We have to face the facts. We have the government standing there with definite proposals which they intend to embody in legislation; proposals which mean, co-terminus with hours, leaving us twelve months time to build up our bargaining power by which we can make demands we cannot make at this moment. What else have we got? Nothing at the moment. . .

The alternative if this conference rejects these proposals means massacre; it means destruction without any protection for our men. The government has not let us down. They will do it as well as we should have done it. We shall have kept the wages. We should not have gone to the government except for our weakness industrially. We asked the government to do something which we could not do ourselves. That is our only protection.

The conference voted by 346 votes to 186 to accept the government proposals; there was no other practical alternative.

What of Cook's leadership during these months? He was praised by *The Times*, criticised by Ablett, vilified by the CPGB, and was publicly defending the none too spectacular efforts of the government. Yet surely his leadership represented a consistent and realistic response to the MFGB's position. What does seem to have been different about Cook at this time, however, was the lack of emotion in his speeches. If ever there was an opportunity for impassioned oratory surely these months of poverty and suffering presented it. Perhaps Cook wished to provide the miners with as clear-headed and pragmatic leadership as possible, mindful of the criticism levelled at him after 1926. Perhaps he deliberately suppressed his anger and frustration, expressed in his private letter to MacDonald, in order to retain a productive relationship with the Cabinet. It is also possible that his painful illness was reducing his ability to carry the burden of mass suffering. It is feasible that by July cancer had been diagnosed, and Cook may well have begun to adopt the mild and genial mood which he was to display during the last three months of his life.

His last article was written for the *Labour Magazine*; it has a resigned, sad, almost nostagic feel to it. Yet it was certainly the work of a committed socialist, one who cared deeply about the miners and their families. Cook, however, played no further part in the MFGB's efforts to improve miners' living standards. Throughout 1930 and 1931 Cook made several visits to Geneva, where the International Labour Organisation of the League of Nations was discussing a uniform working-day for the coal industry. Returning from one of these visits, Cook caught a severe cold and became ill. It was discovered he had sarcoma, a form of cancer. Even today, sarcoma normally results in death within two to three years; in the 1930s life expectancy must have been considerably shorter. Cook apparently kept the nature of his illness secret, even from his wife. In September he attended the Trades Union Congress in Bristol, against doctor's orders, and there he informed a *Western Mail* reporter that he knew he was 'for it'.[18] On 15 September *The Times* reported that Cook had accepted an invitation from the National Union of Seamen to stay at their convalescent home in Surrey, as his health had 'not recovered since the operation he had eight months ago'. Instead, however, Cook was forced to re-enter hospital for urgent treatment of swollen glands and lung problems. On 27 September Cook underwent a neck operation, presumably to remove a cancerous growth.

Knowing his death was imminent, and suffering considerable pain, Cook seems to have lost his last reserves of militancy. In autobiographical notes written for the TUC archives Cook stated that he had been a member of the ILP for twenty-five years, 'where I have always worked in order to assist the Labour Party'.[19] There was no mention of his syndicalist beliefs, his membership of the CPGB, and his association with the Minority Movement. All sources of controversy (and there had been many) were ignored. These notes seem to be the attempt of a dying man to make peace with the past. Cook had usually been on friendly terms in private with Labour leaders he had clashed with publicly. Walter Citrine, for example was a close acquaintance; Arthur Horner mended his differences with his long-time friend and visited him in hospital. Ben Tillett, who had traded harsh words with Cook in the past, was probably the last union leader to see him alive.

During the night of 19 October Cook's condition deteriorated rapidly. His sister Louise, who was a frequent visitor to the Manor House Hospital during these last months, recalled that: 'At the time when he was ill, in all the conversations I had with him, there was no bitterness or hardness in his heart about the hardships of the miners. I never heard him talk about that then.'[20] Shortly after the Labour Party's electoral rout of 27 October, Ben Tillett visited Cook and later revealed that

> He was terribly agitated about the Labour Party's collapse in the election, and said to me, 'What has happened to the multitude to desert you and other old friends like this?' I tried to soothe him, and assured him that the cause was not dead, and would rise again. He grasped my hand and held it for about ten minutes, saying beseechingly, 'Don't go, old man. Don't leave me.' Then he seemed to pause a little, and murmured, 'Goodbye, Ben.' I left him then, knowing that the end was very near.[21]

Cook's condition remained critical for several days, and in the early hours of 2 November he passed away. Apparently his last words were to the nurse who was watching over him – it was a cold night, and he told her to go and warm herself; she returned to find him dead.

Arthur Cook was cremated at Golders Green on 5 November. Tributes were paid by many colleagues. Perhaps the most eloquent was provided by Ernest Bevin:

I know of no man in the Miners' Federation who had fought so hard and yet created such an extraordinary love for himself in the hearts of miners as Arthur Cook. He was abused probably more than any other man of this generation, and yet all the time he worked and fought, guided by the highest motives.

The small chapel in the crematorium was packed with family, friends and colleagues during the service. Outside in the fog, as the mourners emerged to the strains of the 'Dead March', a large crowd sang 'The Red Flag' and 'The Internationale'.

8   Conclusions

Arthur Cook died just twenty days before his forty-eighth birthday. So ended one of the briefest and yet most remarkable careers in labour history. He had been Secretary of the MFGB for just seven years, and yet so much had been crammed into that period that he seems to have occupied the spotlight of the trade union world for much of that time. In this final short chapter some important conclusions will be drawn concerning the character of Cook's leadership.

No amount of sober analysis can diminish the essentially emotional nature of Cook's appeal. The weight of opinion, among his friends and colleagues, contemporary observers and historians, is that Cook's intellectual attributes were outshone by his ability to rouse and motivate the miners. Will Lawther, who knew Cook as early as 1911 when they attended the Central Labour College together, stated that Cook was 'simply a propagandist'.[1] James Griffiths, a young miners' agent in the anthracite district of South Wales in the 1920s, but destined to become President of the SWMF and a member of the Labour Cabinet after the Second World War, thought that Cook 'was an evangelist, Cook was not a negotiator, if you like he was not a compromiser'.[2] Francis Williams, a contemporary fortunate enough to have witnessed Cook, described him as 'a mountain torrent, a man governed almost wholly by emotion. He was an agitator on the grand scale; the propagandist incarnate containing within himself all the passionate sense of injustice that had bitten deep into the hearts of the miners for generations'.[3] David Kirkwood, one of the Clydeside MPs close to Cook in 1928, thought the miners' leader to be an 'agitator, pure and simple'.[4] And Beatrice Webb, of course, in her diary, dismissed Cook as an 'inspired idiot'.[5] Contemporaries who knew Cook well also concluded that Cook's leadership was based on emotion. Robin Page Arnot, for example, recounted that

> He was unlike any other trade union General Secretary, who has to learn the technique of administration, the minute detail of the office work, the habit of cautious speech in negotiations with employers or government departments. When a highly placed government official visited Cook on some delicate or intricate problem, he would harangue for a whole hour on the grievances of the miners and simply ignore the particular problem or any matter that was beyond his compass: and the Cabinet emissary would have to retire, baffled.[6]

And even Cook's closest friend, Arthur Horner, felt that Cook 'wasn't a logical thinker. He wasn't a good negotiator. He was absolutely undisciplined.'[7]

Not surprisingly, historians have echoed the picture of Cook as an emotional firebrand. Generations of history students have had a one-dimensional picture of Cook as 'fiery', 'a Communist', a man lacking all inclinaton to compromise or negotiate. It seems to have been sufficient to use the 'not a penny off the pay. . .' slogan and Cook's famous declaration that ' I don't care a hang for any government or army or navy. . .' and let readers draw the obvious conclusions.[8]

Cook, of course, was 'a firebrand' – full of passion, intensity, anger and an acute sense of injustice which drove him on. At times he was reckless and unstable. Cook possessed qualities which were not normally associated with sound and sensible trade union leadership. He seemed to be a throwback to the days when union officials tended to be propagandists rather than administrators. Cook was an evangelical campaigner who intoxicated his mining audiences with emotion. He was loved and admired by the miners because he mirrored their desires. He spoke for them not to them, as Horner understood. And yet it is hoped that this book has revealed Cook to be something more than an emotional extremist.

Cook was a trade union leader, not the head of a revolutionary sect. He had the same basic responsibilities as other national union secretaries. He had to work within the same limitations. And as Hobsbawm has observed: 'even the most revolutionary must fight the battles for improvement and reform according to the nature of the terrain, which is that of "realistic" calculation in a capitalist economy and a capitalist state. That is to say they must compromise, make allies, and in general act as reformists.'[9] As we have seen, Cook attempted – probably more than any other national leader of his generation – to relate his day-to-day strategy to his long-term ambitions. He believed trade unions were instruments for major social change. Nevertheless, Cook was acutely aware of the need to match policies to their context – that circumstances determine action. In this, despite a super-ficial image of inconsistency, Cook was firm.

In essence, Cook was a syndicalist for the whole of his career. For a summary of his basic philosophy we need to look no further than *The Miners' Next Step*. Cook believed that trade unions could be converted into revolutionary weapons, and that an aggressive policy towards the coalowners would lead ultimately to workers' control. Even at this early stage in his career, however Cook seems to have clearly understood the need for unity and strength. He believed that the workers and their employers were locked in a perpetual struggle, and that no quarter should be asked for or given. Consequently the dictum of the Rhondda syndicalists, 'we can only get what we are strong enough to win and retain', was the keystone of Cook's industrial philosophy.

The miners did not lose a major industrial struggle between 1912 and 1920. The demand for coal was strong, profits were high, and the mining unions were in a strong position to achieve wage increases. During this period Cook was able to match the day-to-day struggle for better working conditions to the syndicalist ambition to expropriate profit and seize control. The year 1921, however, was a violent turning-point in the fortunes of the mining industry. From this point onwards Cook's actions had less to do with revolutionary ambitions than with a desperate struggle to protect miners' living standards. The defeat of 1921 revealed the extent to which Cook was prepared to recognise the need to retreat as well as attack. In the dismal aftermath of that dispute he was even prepared to co-operate with coalowners in an effort to improve employment opportunities. This short period was perhaps the only time when Cook took action which was incongruous with his fundamental beliefs, and can be contrasted to his refusal to tolerate attempts to foster industrial peace with employers after 1926. His reaction to the 1921 defeat reveals the extent to which his basic humanitarianism led him to compromises which he believed were in the immediate interests of the men and families he represented. The failure of his moderate policy served to confirm his opinion of the coalowners and the need to rebuild the miners' forces, and he returned to a militant stance. But in one respect, as in many others, 1921 was a foretaste of what happened during the 1926 lock-out – Cook reacted desperately to defeat and the suffering of the mining communities, and it drove him to actions which had more to do with panic than planning. And yet those actions, even the policy of co-operation after 1921, have a fundamental logic to them: to Cook they were necessary responses to prevailing conditions.

Throughout 1925 and the early months of 1926 Cook's strategy was based on his belief in the inevitability of conflict to protect miners' wages and hours. The defeat of 1921 had convinced him that the miners alone could not win a battle against the coalowners and a hostile government. His efforts, both in conferences and mass meetings, was to improve the miners' strength and bargaining position. His oratory was of course designed to bolster union membership and encourage a spirit of resistance within mining villages. The failure of the General Strike quickly led Cook to recommend compromise. At first he restricted this advice to private meetings, believing that to show signs of weakness to his public audiences would have damaged morale and worsened the miners' position. But one of the myths that surround Cook is the belief that he adhered blindly to the 'not a penny off the pay, not a second on the day' policy. Indeed, during negotiatons with the government and the Mining Association, Cook provided the MFGB's most realistic leadership. The gradual decline of the miners' fighting strength sapped Cook's spirit, and in the gloom of impending defeat he searched anxiously for a settlement. His negotiations with Rowntree and Layton reveal his willingness to compromise. Here again, however, fear of defeat added to tremendous physical and mental strain, produced desperation. Paradoxically, the solidarity of the miners which Cook had done so much to encourage meant that his advice regarding compromise was rejected by the lodges. Meanwhile the intransigence of the coalowners and Cabinet left Cook with little room to manoeuvre.

The crushing defeat of 1926 robbed the miners of their industrial power. As a result Cook's syndicalist dreams lay in tatters. The period between the lock-out and his death saw Cook struggle to find a workable strategy which suited conditions of poverty, demoralisation and industrial impotence. His campaign against the Mond–Turner talks and his alliance with the Clydesiders are evidence of his continued commitment to militant ideas, but he soon realised that the only hope of a short-term improvement in miners' conditions lay with the election of a Labour Government. His support for Labour in 1929-31 was not born out of moral or physical decline – it was a logical consequence of the MFGB's weakness. His renewed membership of the ILP was not so much a philosophical rejection of syndicalism but the formal recognition that reliance on union strength was no longer the most effective approach. Cook's ability to alter tactics to suit conditions had been a quality appreciated by his friend Horner back in 1924, and it should not be confused with instability. Throughout his career Cook advocated as radical a policy as he believed circumstances allowed. This philosophy implied flexibility. Far from being simply an agitator, Cook was capable of formulating pragmatic strategies. In its obituary to Cook, the MFGB Executive observed that

> During his period of office, the economic circumstances of the industry made his job an exceedingly difficult one. While these circumstances tended to reveal in a clearer light than before the soundness of the Federation policy in relation to the economic position of the coal industry, they made decisions in respect of wages and hours of far greater importance than in normal times.
>
> When the industry is in a precarious state; when it is undergoing a process of change and readaption, an unwise decision on these matters may ultimately have far-reaching cnsequences to the men. At such times, even more than in normal times, it becomes vitally necessary to preserve a proper balance between that which is desirable, and that which is economically possible in the circumstances of the moment.
>
> The one great desire of our late Secretary's life was to advance *both the immediate and the ultimate welfare of the men he represented*, and his sincerity and whole-hearted devotion to their cause won the admiration of men in every walk of life.

Cook, of course, had faults and weaknesses. Compared with Ablett, Horner and Bevan – the most intellectually gifted Labour leaders to emerge from the South Wales coalfield – Cook appears unsophisticated, a man of instinct rather than ideology. His thoughts and energy were absorbed by day-to-day actions. Even in his carefully-written articles and pamphlets he was unable to discuss problems facing the Labour movement with the same grasp of theory that Ablett and others were able to command. Cook also failed to realise that the attraction he drew to himself by his sensational speeches was a double-edged sword. By 1926 the coalowners, government ministers and the press were able to point to Cook's outbursts as evidence of fanaticism which must be crushed. Cook seems to have taken a perverse delight in the adverse comments he drew from his opponents, but perhaps he failed to appreciate the damage it did to the miners' cause in the eyes of the public and some sections within the Labour movement. It is also possible to point to the 1926 dispute as evidence of Cook's inability to cope with the strains of crisis. In those desperate days the job of the MFGB Secretary was big enough without the added burden of public-speaking campaigns. Cook's passion and sympathy for the miners led him to attempt too much. The result was exhaustion and near breakdown – circumstances which cannot have helped the effectiveness of his leadership.

But these faults pale into insignificance compared to his qualities. His integrity was never questioned, nor was his sincerity and devotion to the miners' cause. As Page Arnot wrote, 'Today his faults are forgotten or forgiven amongst the older miners who tell the younger men their recollection of past days; and still, in every colliery village, there abides the memory of a great name'.[10] Fenner Brockway has written:

> He was loved by his men, who sensed his utter sincerity and who heard in his words their own thoughts expressed which sent them back to their struggle with new determination. Someone once said that A. J. Cook never knew what he was going to say before he got

on a platform, what he was saying whilst he was on a platform, and what he said when he got down from a platform. There was some truth in this, but it did not matter greatly because Arthur Cook had the right stuff in him and nothing but the right stuff could come out of him.[11]

And perhaps the last word should be left to Cook's closest friend and the man who knew him best, Arthur Horner: 'the other factors he lacked didn't matter – he was the voice of the miners – the depressed miners. I think he was a very great man.'

Appendix: Cook and the secret negotiations of July 1926

Anxious to achieve a settlement of the coal dispute, and taking advantage of the wider scope for negotiations afforded by the government's declared intention to restore an eight-hour day, Seebohm Rowntree and Walter Layton began to explore avenues of possible agreement. Rowntree's private secretary, F. D. Stuart, met Vernon Hartshorn and Frank Hodges on 28 June. Hodges complained that the government's decision to introduce an Eight Hours Act left moderate miners' leaders little room to maneouvre: 'we have either to support Cook or keep quiet'.[1] Hartshorn urged Stuart to see Cook, which Stuart did the following day, presenting himself as a private individual. Apparently Cook was anxious to re-open negotiations and told Stuart that 'if some big captains of industry outside the coal industry could intervene they might be able to bring about a settlement'.[2] Stuart persuaded Cook to meet Rowntree and Layton, and the meeting took place on the afternoon of Friday 2 July. The MFGB Secretary gave the impression he wanted a lasting peace based on the Samuel Report, on condition the Eight Hours Bill was dropped. After Cook had left them the intermediaries went to see Sir Horace Wilson, Permanent Secretary at the Ministry of Labour. Wilson was not particularly impressed, revealing that earlier attempts to involve Cook in unofficial discussions had proved unproductive. Rowntree and Layton persevered, however, and drafted a proposed agreement based on their discussions with Cook and Wilson. Stuart then contacted Cook on the evening of 2 July and persuaded him to meet Rowntree and Layton once more that night. According to Layton Cook then actually met Wilson, although he had at first been unwilling to meet a government representative for fear the discussions would become too formal. Cook's evidence submitted to the MFGB investigators in 1928 did not mention a meeting with Wilson, and neither did the MFGB Executive's subcommittee report. The Ministry of Labour's own diary of negotiations also fails to record any meeting between Cook and Wilson.[3] Layton, however, stated that Cook agreed to see Wilson on condition the meeting was kept secret. At the meeting Cook voiced agreement with the terms drawn up by the intermediaries, although he insisted that no reference should be made to longer hours. Cook signed nothing at this stage, however. According to Rowntree and Stuart, Cook was already 'in a state of extreme exhaustion, and one felt in discussing with him that he was almost at the end of his tether. Indeed, it seemed almost cruelty to get him to think.'[4] On the following day, 3 July, Cook took off for the West Midlands coalfield. Aware that the MFGB Secretary's signature was required before the government would even consider reviewing its policy, Stuart followed Cook to Staffordshire. At Cannock Chase he caught up with him and pressed him to sign the document embodying the intermediaries' proposals. Stuart assured Cook that the document was 'private and secret', and for the 'sole purpose of holding the Eight Hours Bill and securing the opening of negotiations between the government and the Miners' Federation', adding that if he did sign Rowntree and Layton hoped the Eight Hours Bill would be dropped. Cook then signed, adding a footnote and a covering letter:

Document 1: The Rowntree-Layton Proposals signed by A. J. Cook, 3 July 1926
1. Conference to meet to arrive at agreed interpretation of Report – including question of stage to which reorganization proposals

should be carried before any wage changes that may be required in conformity with the Report become operative.

2. Conference to be in first instance between two sides and the Government. Failing agreement, interpretation to be left to Samuel (or Commission). Decisions as to interpretation to be reached within four weeks (or other agreed period).

3. Parties to agree in advance to put into effect the whole Report as interpreted by the Conference.

4. Conference to endeavour to estimate financial results of reorganization and the wages problems will be discussed in the light of these estimates.

5. The Conferenece will endeavour to reach an agreement, both as to the wages to be paid in the period, following the time limit and as to the permanent machinery for wage fixation.

6. Present subsistence rates not to be altered except by mutual agreement or recourse to the machinery already used for the purpose of fixing them.

7. If the Conference cannot agree during its deliberations as to the readjustment of wages to come into effect at the end of the time limit, the question to be remitted to a wages board – as contemplated by the Report – containing a neutral element with power to determine the necessary readjustments as from the end of the time limit contemplated in paragraph 2.

(The permanent machinery of wage fixation must not be on the basis of compulsory arbitration – i.e. the men will not be asked to surrender the right to strike. But the machinery would not necessarily exclude voluntary arbitration. If, however, the machinery includes the right of rejecting arbitration in any particular controversy, the wages fixed in accordance with this paragraph must be valid for a period to be fixed in advance.)

8. Men to resume work forthwith on April terms, any losses during the period fixed in accordance with paragraph 2 may be made good, either by a loan secured as a first charge on the total proceeds of the industry or by some subsequent readjustment of the proceeds of the industry (recoupment).

9. With a view to increasing output and so reducing the cost of production, the Miners' Federation will undertake:

(a) to co-operate in a scheme to deal with voluntary absenteeism, if necessary by penalties;

(b) to ensure the working of the full shifts in Durham (and Northumberland);

(c) to work double shifts in South Wales or any other area in which it is practicable and is desired by the Owners;

(d) to discourage any restriction of output and to co-operate in the establishment and full utilization of machinery to settle any question of alleged restriction;

(e) to assist in the extention to us as many grades as possible of the principle of piecework or some other system of payments by results.

Appended Note (emphasis in original)
I am prepared, speaking for myself, on condition that the government do not proceed with their Hours Bill, to recommend my officials and Executive to consider these proposals as a basis for discussion.

(signed) A. J. Cook
3 July 1926

Document 2: Covering letter signed by A. J. Cook on 3 July 1926
I want to make a very strong appeal that the proposals which I have agreed to support shall be seriously considered as an alternative to the Hours Bill. I do not make the statement as a threat, but I am perfectly certain that if the Hours Bill goes through, it will create an insurmountable obstacle to negotiations. Even if the owners succeed, as they hope to do, in forcing the men back to work on the terms of the Eight Hours Bill, they would create a situation which would mean, for many years to come, a bitter struggle to restore the seven hours. There will thus be a rallying point for agitation until that Bill is repealed, and there will be no rest and no goodwill in the industry. Moreover the Miners' Federation will have the whole Trade Union Movement behind it in its agitation

for the repeal of the Act. On the other hand, if the Government will accept the proposals herewith put forward as an alternative to the passing of the Act, *as a basis for discussion,* the Miners' Federation will do everything they possibly can to increase output and to develop machinery for securing permanent peace and good will. In a word the alternatives for the coal trade are: 'Five years' peace, or five years' unrest'.

A. J. Cook

Rowntree and Layton were disappointed that Cook had added the significant qualification *'as a basis for discussion'*. Rowntree noted later: 'Directly I saw the addition I realized that it amounted to very little. . . This doesn't tie him at all.'[6] It is not certain, therefore, that Cook was prepared to accept the terms in the document in return for a settlement on the lines of the Samuel Report. Certainly the proposals in clause 9 would have been major concessions: increased output in circumstances of over-production was contrary to Cook's and the MFGB's analysis of the coal crisis. Cook was a firm opponent of the piece-work system, and he was obviously aware of the South Wales miners' traditional opposition to the double-shift system. Nevertheless, the fact that Cook was prepared to sign his name to such proposals even as a basis for discussion, reveals his frantic anxiety to prevent a longer working day and open a channel of escape from the crushing defeat which the MFGB faced.

On 4 July Cook made the following statement during a speech in Wigan:

there could not and would not be any negotiations on the question of longer hours. The miners would meet the Government at any time they withdrew the Bill. They would discuss a wages agreement, but they wanted it discussed when their men returned to work on the 'status quo'. Then they promised that they would set up machinery.

By this time, however, the government had embraced a policy

involving longer hours, and was unwilling to return to a settlement based on the Samuel Report – a course which would involve
the government in some reorganisation of the coal industry. On
4 July Rowntree and Layton saw Steel-Maitland, who told them:
'it would be difficult for him to persuade the Cabinet to hold
up the (Eight Hours) Bill without something more definite.' The
Minister of Labour also informed them they were 'about the fifth
set of intermediaries that have been at work, and every time it
came to making some definite undertaking, Cook jibbed'.[7] On
the following day Steel-Maitland confirmed that 'Mr Cook's present formula did not go far enough to justify the Government
holding up the Bill.' The Minister also suggeset a further clause
– 7a – which would allow longer hours:

> Document 3: Clause 7a, drafted on 5 July 1926
> 7a. If, after taking into account the financial results of reorganization
> referred to in paragraph 4, the Wages Board finds itself compelled
> by the conditions prevailing in a particular district to fix wage rates
> other than those of men on the subsistence minimum substantially
> below the present minimum or alternatively at less than 25 per cent
> above standard, the Board may propose an alternative either no
> change or a smaller reduction in wages rates, combined with an
> increase of hours, provided that the alternative of increased hours
> shall only come into effect if on a ballot in the district concerned
> 66 per cent of the miners voting express their preference for that
> alternative.[8]

Rowntree and Layton tried to persuade Cook to convene a meeting of his Executive to which he would recommend the proposals.
According to the evidence elicited by the MFGB's investigating
subcommittee in 1928, Stuart followed Cook to Holywell and
attempted to persuade him to return to London for this purpose.
Apparently Cook was nervously distraught and broke down and
cried.[9] Cook did return on the night train, however (Stuart
claimed he travelled with Cook), and apparently fixed a meeting

with the intermediaries at the MFGB headquarters for 9.30 a.m. When Layton and Stuart arrived at Russell Square, however, they found that Cook had flown to Berlin to join W. P. Richardson and collect funds from the Russian miners' union. In his testimony in 1928 Cook said he did not remember travelling back to London with Stuart, and that he could not have made arrangements for a 9.30 meeting because his flight to Berlin had been booked in advance.[10] Layton, however, believed that Cook – whom he said had been 'showing signs of extreme fatigue' – had simply forgotten about his flight when fixing the meeting.[11] Steel-Maitland concluded that Cook 'was purposely trying to get time for negotiations to materialise', but Rowntree and Layton felt he had simply abandoned hope of re-opening negotiations.[12] Cook in fact stated later that he rejected clause 7a, and that he did not even see it until he returned from Berlin in 9 July, after the Eight Hours Bill had become law.[13]

With Cook in Germany, Stuart, Rowntree and Layton turned their attention to Herbert Smith. Stuart travelled to Barnsley to interview the MFGB President: there Smith was informed of the talks with Cook and shown a copy of the 3 July document. According to Stuart, Smith remarked: 'If the young man has signed that, I will not let him down'.[14] In a letter to Layton on 21 December 1928, however, Smith denied making such a statement and claimed he would have nothing to do with the document and its terms.[15] But Stuart reported that Smith merely criticised some points and refused to sign his name or recommend it to his Executive. The intermediaries were certainly willing to persevere following Stuart's meeting with the MFGB President, and attempted to have the Eight Hours Bill's passage through parliament delayed. In fact the modern biographers of Baldwin have claimed that the prime minister and Steel-Maitland did indeed hold up the Bill by at least one day.[16] In the end, however, the go-betweens admitted defeat. On 8 July Stuart wrote to

Smith explaining that the Bill could be delayed no further, and complained that 'wherever you had changed the memorandum of which Cook approved, you had made it more difficult to apply it as an instrument in persuading the Government to hold up the Bill'.[17] Smith, however, in claiming he gave no consideration to the 3 July proposals, also denied receiving Stuart's letter.[18] But clearly, if the intermediaries' testimony is accepted with regard to Cook, Herbert Smith himself was also guilty of failing to keep his Executive informed of possible avenues of negotiation.

Upon his return from Berlin Cook was seen by Stuart, who claimed he elicited a promise that Cook would inform his Executive of all that had gone on during the previous fortnight's covert discussion. Apparently Stuart stayed up all night preparing twenty-six copies of the 3 July document (and clause 7a) for the Executive's perusal. In his evidence given in 1928, however, Cook made the logical observation that since the Eight Hours Bill had become law 'there could be no possible purpose in putting copies before the Committee. As far as my recollection goes I neither received nor even saw the copies.'[19] On 14 July the intermediaries tried to see Cook but were informed that he had been called to a meeting of great importance. Cook was in fact taking part in a preliminary meeting of the MFGB officials and representatives of the Christian Churches. The churchmen were prepared to draft proposals for a settlement which were more generous to the miners than those embodied in the Rowntree–Layton document. In fact the 'Bishops' Proposals' included a return to work on pre-stoppage conditions, a national agreement, financial assistance from the government, reorganisation, and compulsory arbitration regarding matters of dispute. Rowntree and Layton were close enough to the government to know that such terms would not be granted, and attempted to reach further agreement with Cook. But they reported finding him 'unwilling to return to the same frame of mind he had been in on 3 July' following the Bishops' intervention.[20] On 21 Layton saw Tom Jones, the Cabinet Secretary, and complained about the churchmen's interference, wishing they would 'go back to look after their flocks'.[21] Rowntree, Layton and Stuart kept in close touch with Cook but with the Bishops' Proposals so popular with the MFGB Secretary and his Executive, their initiatives floundered. When Stuart met Cook on 30 July the miners' leader was 'in one of his flurried moods, and hardly knew which way to turn or what he was saying. . . He told me he had been trounced for going as far as he had in search of peace.'[22] And with the MFGB lodges' rejection of the Bishops' Proposals, Cook was unable to return to any discussion of terms which were less favourable than those presented by the churchmen.

II

Cook's negotiations with Sir Stephen Demetriadi, the Chairman of the London Chamber of Commerce, are not as well documented as the Cook-Rowntree talks, but with one or two logical assumptions a feasible scenario can be formed.

On 19 July Demetriadi wrote to Baldwin, though the letter was dealt with by Steel-Maitland as the prime minister was busy conducting negotiations with the Bishops.

Document 4: Demetriadi to Baldwin, 19 July 1926[23]

Dear Mr Baldwin,

I enclose a copy of a letter which, so far as I can gather, Mr A. J. Cook and his colleagues are prepared to sign and address to me.

It is impossible to speak definitely regarding any possible action by the Miners' Federation but I may say that the letter is the outcome of conversations and discussions between Mr Cook and myself and that I have Mr Cook's personal assurance that he favours the proposals which it contains and does not anticipate objection on the part of his colleagues.

The intention of the letter is twofold:

(1) to get the men back to the mines forthwith.

(2) to ensure at the eariest possible date a reasonable settlement for a period of years.

You will observe that clauses 6 and 7 involve an allowance by Government during the sitting of the Board and Tribunal which is limited to four weeks altogether. This would not be a heavy price to pay for the immediate return of the men to the mines and for a settlement which will obviate a further disturbance of the coal industry for some years to come. However, this is a matter which the Government alone can decide.

The position at present is, that Mr Cook will meet his colleagues to consider and, I believe, to sign this draft provided I can give him a verbal assurance that His Majesty's Government, upon receipt of the signed letter, are prepared to take steps with a view to the setting up of the machinery indicated.

Will you very kindly let me know whether I may give Mr Cook and his colleagues the assurace they require.

In view of the Bishops' deputation to you this evening I think it well to let you know the result, so far, of the discussions I have had with Mr Cook over a period of time and as recently as Friday afternoon.

Yours sincerely,
(signed) Stephen Demetriadi

Document 5: Demetriadi–Cook terms, undated and unsigned
Dear Sir Stephen Demetriadi,

I have given careful consideration to the suggestions you make, and shall be prepared to advise the men to return to work without delay, upon the following terms:

1. The owners and ourselves to attend before a Board which shall endeavour to reach a settlement upon the lines of the Royal Commission's Report.

2. The Board to be presided over by a Chairman, whose functions shall be those of a negotiator.

3. Points upon which no agreement is reached to be referred by the Board to a Tribunal of three persons who shall be experienced in the handling of industrial concerns, but who shall not be connected with the Coal Industry.

4. The Chairman of the Tribunal to be acceptable to both sides, and each side to appoint one of the remaining members.

5. The decision of the Tribunal upon any disputed point to be accepted by both sides as final.

6. The government to guarantee wages at pre-strike rates until the Tribunal has given its decision upon every point referred to it by the Board.

7. The Board shall complete the hearing of all points in dispute within three weeks of
(the resumption of work in the mines
(its first meeting
and the Tribunal shall issue its findings within one week thereafter.

The effect of this proposal would be to leave the vexed questions of hours and wages to the Board, and, in the last result, to the Tribunal, and the Owners shall undertake pending this decision to leave these questions in abeyance.

In short, we are prepared to reach a settlement within the limits of the Coal Commission's Report, if the Government will furnish the strictly impartial machinery I indicate, and will guarantee that the owners, equally with ourselves, will accept the decisions of the Tribunal as binding, for a period of years.

Yours very truly

Steel-Maitland did not place the proposals before Baldwin, and decided that while the terms 'marked a very considerable advance upon any that had hitherto been put forward', Cook's signature would be required before the government could act.[24] The terms, in that they involved binding arbitration on all matters but had no mention of reorgansation, were worse to the miners than those proposed by Rowntree and Layton, and were far less generous than the Bishops' proposals. It seems certain the Demetriadi–

Cook terms were drafted before the churchmen's intervention, and it seems the Bishops' appearance put paid to Cook's interest in these unofficial discussions with Sir Stephen. Before the end of July Demetriadi had informed Steel-Maitland that his proposals were in abeyance while the MFGB negotiated with the Bishops.[25] On 29 July the MFGB Executive decided to support the Bishops' proposals and recommend them to the districts, and at the MFGB's Special Conference the following day Cook spoke in support of his Executive's policy. Thereafter no more was heard of the Demetriadi terms.

The government's unwillingness to provide a subsidy, and their general acceptance of the coalowners' demands, would have prevented the Cook–Demetriadi terms from assuming a central role in the search for a settlement. Ironically, the government's intractability may have saved Cook from great embarrassment – for although he did not sign the draft proposals, if the government had seized upon them and contacted the MFGB Cook would have found himself in very hot water. His support for clauses which allowed for binding arbitration amounted to a major aberration on Cook's part. Perhaps he hoped an independent tribunal chairman might advise settlement on the lines of the Samuel Report (i.e. on a seven-hour day). With the MFGB's bargaining power weakening by the day Cook no doubt felt that was a risk worth taking. It is equally plausible to speculate, however, that Cook's mind was not working clearly – that nervous anxiety and exhaustion had produced a condition where he was not quite sure what repercussions his secret discussions might have. In the event, of course, the government's improving strategic position encouraged it to press for concessions that Cook simply could not contemplate. The Bishops' intervention, meanwhile, offered Cook the opportunity to probe open avenues for a more generous settlement. In effect, Rowntree and Layton's, Demetriadi's, and the churchmen's mediations served to widen the gulf between

Cook and the government.

III

The Cook–Demetriadi negotiations remained secret – much to Arthur Cook's relief, no doubt. But in 1928 his dealings with Rowntree, Layton and Stuart were brought into the open. Apparently Joseph Jones, the Yorkshire miners' leader, had known about Cook's involvement as early as November 1926, but chose to publicise the matter at the height of the struggle within the MFGB between right and left wings. Following Jones's allegations during a speech at Llandudno, a MFGB Executive subcommittee was appointed to investigate. In October 1928 this subcommittee reached the following findings:

1. That on 3 July 1926 Mr Cook did sign a document.
2. That when he did so, he knew that the said document would receive the considerations of the Government departments.
3. That Mr Cook was in possession of at least one copy (from which others could have been struck) which he could have brought before his E.C. at any time between July 6th and the holding of the Bishop's Conference.

As to what the document contains, as to whether it should have been signed, as to whether, when signed, it should have been brought before the E.C., and as to whether it did contain the terms of a settlement or the evasion of the Eight Hours Act, we make no comment, as we do not consider these questions to be within the scope of our inquiry.[26]

In his defence, Cook claimed that at first he had forgotten the entire incident, and stated that he 'met many people and was anxious to meet anybody who could help us, and was prepared to do almost anything to stop the Eight Hours Bill becoming law'.[27] Cook said he was not aware the intermediaries had had a direct entrée to the government, merely influence with 'friends of the government'. He also pointed out: 'it was not competent for me to put any proposals before the Committee other than those of an official character. Many other proposals were submitted to me by other individuals and doubtless many other leaders had similar experiences.'[28] Cook, however, had been in a position to mention the proposals informally to his colleagues, and perhaps even involve them in his dealings with Rowntree and Layton. His pessimism regarding the outcome of the mediation following the introduction of clause 7a, a shortage of time imposed by his visit to Berlin and the imminence of the Bill becoming law, added to Cook's nervous fatigue and probable fear that he had gone too far and would be traduced by his Executive, all tended to inhibit Cook. Arthur Horner stated that Cook had 'had proposals from all over the place and most of them involved some form of capitulation. . . Cook never even told me about them and did not regard them as serious'.[29] But this explanation, as Dr Griffin has pointed out, is not sufficient.[30] It seems far more likely, in fact, that Cook was tired, distraught and desperate: afraid of the Mining Association's and government's intransigence, and fearful for the survival of the MFGB. Moreover, he was acutely aware of the suffering that was occurring in many mining communities. Under such circumstances he believed it was his duty to explore, however tentatively, opportunities for a compromise settlement.

Bibliographical note

Until recently A. J. Cook had not been studied adequately by Labour historians. A simplistic portrait of him as an unstable extremist has emerged, often built on myths and inaccuracies. Historians of the British miners owe an enormous debt to Robin Page Arnot, whose volumes *The Miners: Years of Struggle* (1953) and *The South Wales Miners, Volume II: 1914-1926* (1975) gave me my first glimpse of A. J. Cook and awakened my interest in him. Page Arnot's writings remain a valuable source, and certainly provide a thorough contextual narrative for all subsequent research into the British miners during the first half of this century. Even Page Arnot, however, neglected to analyse the complexity of Cook and merely emphasised his emotional appeal. Furthermore, Page Arnot dismissed Cook's actions after 1928 simply as the result of a physical decline which provoked the abandonment of Cook's basic principles.

Until the 1970s, the only other published references to Cook of any real value were confined to autobiographies and histories of mining districts. Of the former, Arthur Horner's *Incorrigible Rebel* (1960) of course provided a valuable insight into Cook's character. The studies of two Midland districts, Nottinghamshire and Derbyshire, are useful both for their differing analysis and as evidence of how Cook's activities affected local miners' associations. Dr Griffin's *The Miners of Nottinghamshire 1914-1944* (1962) and his *Mining in the East Midlands 1550-1947* (1971) contain interesting criticism of Cook's leadership during the 1925-6 period. Meanwhile J. E. Williams's *The Derbyshire Miners* (1962) provides a far more sympathetic interpretation of the same events.

In addition to these published works there appeared the first real attempt to write specifically about Cook. This took the form of W. G. Quine's MA thesis, 'A. J. Cook: miners' leader in the General Strike' (Manchester University, 1964), which began to put our knowledge of Cook onto a firmer footing, albeit to a small number of readers.

Only in the early 1970s did an accurate picture of Cook begin to emerge in published writings. Professor Desmarais, in his short article for an American journal, 'Charisma and conciliation: a sympathetic look at A. J. Cook' (*Societas*, Winter 1973), began to explore the various dimensions to Cook's leadership, although this study was largely confined to the 1925-6 period. Shortly afterwards Desmarais and Saville produced an entry on Cook for the *Dictionary of Labour Biography* (Vol III, 1976) which despite its obvious brevity marked a further step forward in our understanding of Cook and knowledge of his career. My own research into Cook's career began in 1975, and this produced one published article, 'The making of A. J. Cook' (*Llafur*, vol II, no. 3, 1978) and my unpublished PhD thesis (Bradford University, 1979).

Notes

Chapter 1

1 For details of Cook's early life I have relied heavily on information supplied to me by the late Miss Louise Cook (sister) in interviews during 1975 and 1976. Arthur Cook's autobiographical articles in *Tit-Bits* magazine during April–May 1926, and his autobiographical notes in the TUC Library (file CT/C), are also very important.

2 D. Smith, 'Wales Through the Looking-Glass', in his (ed.) *A People and A Proletariat*.

3 L. J. Williams, 'The Road to Tonypandy', *Llafur* (The Journal of the Society for the Study of Welsh Labour History), Vol. 1, No, 2, May 1973

4 H. Francis and D. Smith, *The Fed*, p. 13.

5 W. H. Mainwaring Papers, mss minutes of South Wales militants, 29 May 1911.

6 *South Wales Worker*, 5 July 1913.

7 *Rhondda Socialist*, 12 October 1912.

Chapter 2

1 W. F. Hay, *War and the Welsh Miner*.

2 *Porth Gazette*, 3 October 1914.

3 M. G. Woodhouse, 'Rank and File Movements among the miners of South Wales, 1910-26', Oxford University DPhil thesis, 1969.

4 Cook, 'The Great Awakening' in the *Merthyr Pioneer*, 15 April 1916.

5 *Merthyr Pioneer*, 3 March 1917.

6 D. Egan, 'The Swansea Conference of the British Council of Soldiers' and Workers Delegates, July 1917: reactions to the Russian Revolution of February 1917, and the anti-war movement in South Wales', *Llafur*, Summer 1975.

7 Home Office 'File on A. J. Cook' (Public Record Office: HO 45/10743/ 263275). Many of the documents in this file have been published as part of an article by D. Hopkin, 'A. J. Cook in 1916-18', *Llafur*, Vol. 2, No. 3, Summer 1978. A full collection of the documents can be found in my PhD thesis 'A J Cook: a study in trade union leadership', Bradford

University, 1979.

8 HO 'File on A. J. Cook', Dept Chief Constable John Williams to Capt. Lionel Lindsay, 9 February 1918.

9 *Porth Gazette*, 6 October 1917.

10 HO 'File on A. J. Cook', Lindsay to Home Office, 24 November 1917.

11 Cab 24/106/1355, Report on Revolutionary Organisations in the UK, 27 May 1920 (PRO).

12 MFGB Special Conference, 12 March 1920.

13 Cab 24/110/1793, Report on Revolutionary Organisations, 9 September 1920.

Chapter 3

1 MFGB Special Conference, 22 February 1921.

2 *Rhondda Leader*, 14 April 1921.

3 R. Page Arnot, *The Miners: Years of Struggle*, p. 321.

4 *The Times*, 20 June 1921.

5 Cab 24/126/3179, Report on Revolutionary Organisations in the UK, 28 July 1921.

6 A. Horner, *Incorrigible Rebel*, pp. 56-7.

7 MFGB Special Conference, 21 December 1922.

8 Cab 24/162/449, Report on Revolutionary Organisations in the UK, 8 November 1923.

9 Horner, *op. cit.*, pp. 43-4.

10 W. A. Citrine, *Men and Work*, pp. 66-7.

11 R. Page Arnot, *op. cit.*, p. 343.

Chapter 4

1 A. Horner, *op. cit.*, p. 72

2 I. Cox, in '1926 remembered and revealed', *Llafur*, Vol. 2, No. 2, Spring 1977.

3 R. Page Arnot. *op. cit.*, p. 351.

4 D. Smith, *Wales! Wales?*, p. 135.

5 MFGB Special Conference, 27 February 1925.

6 J. Scanlon, *Decline and Fall of the Labour Party*, p. 102.

7 *Sunday Worker*, 15 March 1925.

8 MFGB Special Conference, 20–21 May 1925.

9 PRO: Cab 23/50/39, minutes of Cabinet meeting, 22 July 1925.

10 Citrine, *op. cit.*, p. 142.

11 W. A. Lee, *Thirty Years in Coal*, p. 45.

12 Londonderry Papers, D/Lo/C277, Dillon to Londonderry, 4 August 1925 (Durham County Record Office).

13 D. Marquand, *Ramsay MacDonald*, p. 424.

14 *Derbyshire Times*, 8 August 1925, quoted in J. E. Williams, *The Derbyshire Miners*, p. 689.

15 *The Times*, 24 August 1925.

16 TUC Report, 8 September 1925.

17 J. H. Thomas, *My Story*, pp. 105-6.

18 Speech at Port Talbot, *The Times*, 11 January 1926.

19 TUC General Council SIC minutes, 29 January 1926 (TUC Library).

20 *Sunday Worker*, 31 January 1926.

21 G. A. Phillips, *The General Strike*, p. 88.

22 TUC GC SIC minutes, 26 February 1926.

23 J. Lovell, 'The TUC Special Industrial Committee: January-April 1926', in A. Briggs and J. Saville, *Essays in Labour History 1918-1939*.

24 TUC GC SIC minutes, 5 April 1926.

25 T. Jones, *Whitehall Diary*, Vol. 2 (ed. K. Middlemass), p. 16.

26 K. Martin, *Father Figures*, p. 162.

27 A. J. Cook, *The Nine Days*, p. 16.

28 Phillips, *op. cit.*, p. 151.

29 Citrine, *op. cit.*, p. 194.

30 Samuel Papers, A/157/1082, Samuel to Beatrice Samuel, 14 May 1926 (House of Lords Record Office).

31 Cook, *The Nine Days*, p. 21.

Chapter 5

1 M. W. Kirby, *The British Coalmining Industry, 1870-1946*, p. 97.

2 T. Jones, *Whitehall Diary*, Vol. 2, pp. 60-1.

3 *The Times*, 18 June 1926.

4 W. A. Citrine, *Men and Work*, p. 209.

5 F. Brockway, *Inside the Left*, pp. 193-4.

6 Arthur Horner, cited in D. Smith, 'Leaders and Led', in K. S. Hopkins (ed.), *Rhondda Past and Future*.

7 G. Short, 'The miners fight on', *Marxism Today*, Vol. 20, no. 5, May 1976.

8 Glyn Evans, interviewed by R. Lewis and H. Francis, 5 March 1973 (transcipt in the South Wales Miners' Library).

9 J. Lawson, *The Man in the Cap: the Life of Herbert Smith*, pp. 215-16.

10 *The Times*, 22 June 1926.

11 PRO: Lab 27/3, Coal Dispute, Diary of Negotiations, 25 June 1926.

12 R. H. Desmarias, 'Charisma and conciliation: a sympathetic look at A. J. Cook', *Societas,* Winter 1973, pp. 45-60.

13 A. Briggs, *A Study of the Work of Seebohm Rowntree 1871-1954*, pp. 256-68; PRO: Lab 27/3, Coal Dispute Diary of Negotiations, 2 July 1926.

14 Briggs, *op. cit.*, p. 258.

15 *Ibid.*

16 *The Times*, 5 July 1926.

17 Briggs, *op. cit.*, p. 259.

18 T. Jones, *op. cit.*, p. 62.

19 Briggs, *op. cit.*, p. 259; Steel-Maitland Papers, Diary of Coal Dispute, 5 July 1926 (Scottish Record Office Edinburgh).

20 *The Times*, 10 July 1926.

21 MFGB Special Conference, 30 July 1926.

22 *The Times*, 26, 27 July 1026.

23 *The Times*, 16 August 1926. Cook asked the meeting for a show of hands on the question 'that the policy I have put forward is a real policy for us to pursue, and that it is a policy that should be utilised at the next conference'. This motion was carried with only two dissentients.

24 MFGB Special Conference, 16 August 1926.

25 *The Times*, 24 August 1926; J. E. Williams, *The Derbyshire Miners*, pp. 715-16.

26 Compare this with Lord Birkenhead's telegram to the Cabinet: 'Cook's most recent speech repeats so-called slogans and suggests he is merely making an impudent tactical attempt to save his face.' Jones, *op. cit.*, pp. 68-9.

27 Jones, *op. cit.*, p. 69.

28 MFGB, minutes of meeting between government representatives and the MFGB national officials, 26 August 1926.

29 *Ibid.*

30 Jones, *op. cit.*, p. 69; see also M. Gilbert, *Winston Churchill, Vol. V: 1922-1939*, pp. 183-5.

31 PRO: Lab 27/4, William Brace to Sir Ernest Gowers, 7 September 1926.

32 B. Webb, *Diaries*, pp. 115-17.

33 *The Miner*, 11 September 1926.

34 *The Times*, 27 September 1926.

35 Jones, *op. cit.*, p. 88.

36 *The Times*, 4 October 1926.

37 *The Times*, 9 October 1926.

38 *The Times*, 11 October 1926.

39 Speech at Wigan, *The Times*, 18 October 1926.

40 PRO: Cab 25/53/53, minutes of Cabinet meeting, 18 October 1926.

41 *Ibid*.

42 House of Commons Parliamentary Debates, Vol. 199, cols 637, 639, 641, 25 October 1926.

43 Speech at Liverpool, *The Times*, 8 November 1926.

Chapter 6

1 *The Times*, 22 November 1926.

2 *Ibid*, 29 November 1926.

3 R. H. Desmarais and J. Saville, entry on Cook in J. Bellamy and J. Saville (eds.) *Dictionary of Labour Biography*, Vol. III, pp. 38-44.

4 Phillips, *op. cit.*, p. 259.

5 *The Times*, 7 December 1926.

6 D. F. Calhoun, *The United Front: the TUC and the Russians, 1923-28*, p. 327, quoting Foreign Office reports, FO 371/11803, to Austen Chamberlain.

7 *The Times*, 1 January 1927.

8 See H. Clegg, *A History of British Trade Unions,*, Vol. II, 1911-33, pp. 419-21.

9 Cook to MacDonald, 13 January 1927; MacDonald to Cook, 14 January 1927 (quoted in Marquand, *op. cit.*, p. 448).

10 *Reynold's Illustrated News*, 2 January 1927.

11 Phillips, *op. cit.*, p. 258.

12 *Ibid*, p. 259.

13 R. Martin, *Communism and the British Trade Unions, 1924-33: A Study of the National Minority Movement*, p. 82.

14 M. Jacques, 'Consequences of the General Strike', in J. Skelley (ed.), *The General Strike*.

15 Horner, *op. cit.*, pp. 100-1.

16 *Sunday Worker*, 6 November 1927.

17 R. Charles, *The Development of Industrial Relations in Britain, 1911-1939*, p. 283.

18 A. Bullock, *The Life and Times of Ernest Bevin*, Vol. I, p. 400.

19 Arthur Horner Papers, A/2, Cook to Horner, 10 October 1927 (University College Swansea Library).

20 *Ibid.*, A/3, Cook to Horner, 26 January 1928.

21 D. Smith, 'The struggle against company unionism in the South Wales

21 Coalfield 1926-1939', *Welsh History Review*, June 1973.
22 A. R. and C. P. Griffin, 'The Non-Political Trade Union Movement', in A. Briggs and J. Saville (eds.) *Essays in Labour History 1918-1939*; J. E. Williams, *op. cit.*, p. 740; Horner, *op. cit.*, p. 130; Smith, 'The struggle against company unionism', *op. cit.*
23 ILP, National Administrative Council minutes, 30 June 1928. Moody and Sankey were American religious revivalists and hymn-writers who visited Britain in the 1870s.
24 Cook, speech at St Albans, *The Times*, 22 June 1928.
25 K. Middlemass, *The Clydesiders*, p. 219.
26 Scanlon, *op. cit.*, p. 111.
27 J. McNair, *James Maxton: The Beloved Rebel*, p. 174.
28 G. W. McDonald and H. F. Gospel, 'The Mond–Turner talks 1927-1933: a study in industrial co-operation', *Historical Journal*, 1973.
29 Horner, *op. cit.*, p. 101.

Chapter 7

1 MFGB minutes, 13 September 1928.
2 See, for example, L. J. Macfarlane, *The British Communist Party*, pp. 261-2; R. Martin, *op. cit.*, pp, 119-20; Desmarais and Saville, *op. cit.*; J. Mahon, *Harry Pollitt: A Biography*, p. 150.
3 *The Times*, 13 October 1928.
4 J. Degras (ed.), Soviet Documents on Foreign Policy, Vol II: 1925-1932, p. 237.
5 R. Miliband, *Parliamentary Socialism*, p. 153.
6 *Sunday Worker*, 14 October 1928.
7 Cook, appeal for a miners' relief fund, *Daily Herald*, 18 October 1928.
8 *The Miner*, 9 March 1929.
9 H. Dewar, *Communist Politics in Britain*, p. 95.
10 MFGB, minutes of conference with government representatives, 16 October 1929.
11 *The Miner*, 4 January 1930.
12 R. Skidelsky, *Politicians and the Slump*, p. 47.
13 TUC GC minutes, 22 October 1930.
14 R. Skidelsky, *Oswald Mosley*, p. 255.
15 Ramsay MacDonald Papers, PRO 30/69/2/8, Cook to MacDonald, 9 January 1931 (Public Record Office).
16 *Ibid*, MacDonald to Cook, 12 January 1931.

17 *Ibid*, note from Miss Rosenburg, dated 31 January 1931.
18 *Western Mail*, 3 November 1931.
19 Cook, autobiographical notes, 1931 (no precise date), TUC Library.
20 Louise Cook, interviewed by author, 23 October 1975.
21 *Daily Express*, 3 November 1931.

Chapter 8

1 Sir William Lawther, interviewed by J. F. Clarke, *Bulletin of the Society for the Study of Labour History*, 19, Autumn 1969.
2 James Griffiths, interviewed by R. Lewis and H. Francis, 20 November 1972 (transcript in South Wales Miners Library, Swansea).
3 F. Williams, *Magnificant Journey*, p. 368.
4 D. Kirkwood, *My Life of Revolt*, p. 231.
5 Beatrice Webb, *Diaries op. cit.*, p. 116.
6 R. Page Arnot, *The Miners: Years of Struggle*, pp. 350-1.
7 Arthur Horner, quoted in P. Renshaw, *The General Strike*, p. 100.
8 See, for example, a standard Advanced Level History textbook, L. C. B. Seaman, *Post-Victorian Britain*, 1902-1951, pp. 192-3.
9 E. J. Hobsbawn, 'Trends in the British Labour Movement since 1850', in his *Labouring Men* (1968 edn), pp. 316-43.
10 R. Page Arnot, *The Miners: Years of Struggle*, p. 541.
11 F. Brockway, *Inside the Left*, p. 194.

Appendix

1 Report of F. D. Stuart's interview with Hodges and Hartshorn, 28 June 1926, in Asa Briggs, *A Study of the Work of Seebohm Rowntree 1881-1954*, p. 257.
2 Report of interview between Cook and Stuart, *ibid*.
3 PRO: Lab 27/3, Coal Dispute, Diary of Negotiations, 2 July 1926.
4 Briggs, *op. cit.*, p. 258.
5 *Ibid*; also W. T. Layton, 'Attempted Mediation in the Coal Dispute: Memorandum of Events in the First Fortnight of July 1926', dated 3 November 1928 and presented to the MFGB's investigating subcommittee.
6 Briggs, *op. cit.*, pp. 258-9.
7 Briggs, *op. cit.*, p 259; Steel-Maitland Papers, GD 193/412, Diary of General Strike and Coal Dispute, 4 July 1926 (Scottish Record Office, Edinburgh).
8 Layton, *op. cit.*
9 MFGB, 'Report of Sub-Committee', 22 October 1928.

10 Cook, 'Statement to MFGB Executive', 26 October 1928.

11 Layton, *op. cit.*

12 Briggs, *op. cit.*, p. 259.

13 Cook, 'Statement to MFGB EC'.

14 Briggs, *op. cit.*,, p. 260; Layton, *op. cit.*,

15 MFGB, copy of letter from Smith to Layton, 21 December 1928.

16 Middlemass and Barnes, *Baldwin*, p. 431.

17 MFGB, copy of letter from Stuart to Smith, 8 July 1926. See also Stuart's report of his meeting with Smith, in which Smith was apparently quite enthusiastic about the 3 July terms: Briggs, *op. cit.*, p. 361-2.

18 Smith to Layton, *op. cit.*

19 Cook, 'Statement to MFGB EC'.

20 Briggs, *op. cit.*, p. 263.

21 T. Jones, *Whitehall Diary II*, pp. 62-3.

22 Briggs, *op. cit.*, p. 263.

23 Steel-Maitland Papers, GD 193/109/5.

24 *Ibid.*, Steel-Maitland's Note on Demetriadi's Mediation, 20 July 1926.

25 *Ibid.*, Coal Diary, 29 July 1926.

26 MFGB, 'Report of Sub-Committee'.

27 Cook, 'Statement to MFGB EC'.

28 *Ibid.*

29 Horner, *Incorrigible Rebel*, p. 199.

30 For an unsympathetic view of Cook's behaviour during this episode see A. R. Griffin, *Mining in the East Midlands*, p. 254.

Index